I ♥ CURRY

The best Indian curries you'll ever cook

Anjum Anand

photography by Jonathan Gregson

Quadrille
PUBLISHING

To my daughter Mahi whose smile, laughter and presence bring pure joy to my life

introduction

During the week I wrote this page, I taught a class of 10-year-old boys how to make a chickpea curry. They had no fear, they trusted me and were excited to try their hands at something new. They all listened as I explained what to look for and how to tell when the base of the curry – the 'masala' – was cooked. And then came the moment when I suggested they try the dish; it was so lovely to see their faces light up as they tasted their own cooking. They had no idea how it would turn out, all these unfamiliar ingredients added one after the other and the dish ready to eat in less than half an hour. Surely Indian food isn't so easy to cook? But it is, you just need to get stuck in and watch as the complex flavours add up to more than the sum of their parts. When you are finished and you try the sauce, you will feel just as proud and elated as those boys.

I used to wince when I heard someone call any Indian dish 'a curry'. 'Going for a curry' simply meant eating at an Indian restaurant, and I wondered how such a majestic, broad cuisine could be shrunk down to just one word. To me – and to most Indian people – a 'curry' is simply a dish with lots of sauce or gravy, and might be a term introduced by the British Raj. The spices will change from region to region. So when mum said that our Punjabi family were having chicken curry for dinner, I knew what to expect. For us it meant succulent chicken in a light tomato and onion-based sauce with a north Indian mix of spices: green and black cardamom, cinnamon, bay, cloves and green chillies, finished with garam masala. But a child in Andhra would know her chicken curry was going to be more fiery, with red chillies and a more aromatic spice mix containing fennel and white poppy seeds, while in Mangalore the spices would be toasted before grinding and the dish finished with rich coconut and tangy tamarind.

So when my publishers and I started talking about a book of Britain's favourite curries, as well as a few of my own creations, I got really excited. Curry, in the real sense of the word, is the ultimate comfort food. We then got down to the thorny question of what a curry really is. Our conclusion – and the premise of this book – is that a curry is a stand-alone main course dish, with or without lots of sauce and with or without a dominant spice, that you only need some rice or bread to enjoy.

I've thought a lot about what curries people want to eat. The result is 54 curry recipes, both easy everyday dishes and restaurant classics, plus loads of ideas for starters and accompaniments. Here are all our favourites: chicken tikka masala, lamb do piaza, balti, vindaloo and many, many more. The more adventurous cook will also find lots of exciting new flavours, such as lamb chops with dried pomegranate, or Bengali mustard fish. This is the whole world of curries in all their glory.

It was great fun making up these recipes and I hope you'll find just as much joy in cooking them. Involve friends and/or children – or just put on some great music – and watch and taste the magic come to life… just as it did for those 10-year-old boys.

making great curry: the secrets

The best way to learn a country's cuisine is to cook with a native, because you pick up so many tips that will make the difference between a good dish and a fabulous one. Because not all of us can cook beside an Indian, I want to be a stand-in here for you. I hope to give you a deeper understanding of how to cook a curry and maximise its flavours. So, when you get to the stove, remember these five distinct and vital building blocks…

STAGE 1: whole spices

Always the first ingredient to go into the hot oil. They add a greater depth of flavour than ground spices.

cumin seeds should be fried until they release a nutty aroma and have reddened a couple of shades. It should only take five seconds sizzling in hot oil.
fenugreek seeds should darken to medium brown.
mustard seeds start popping straight away in hot oil. As they pop, reduce the heat and, once the popping dies down, move on to the next stage.
nigella and carom seeds need only about 10 seconds in hot oil to release their full aroma.
other whole spices (cinnamon, cloves, cardamom pods, black pepper etc) should be cooked in hot oil for 20–30 seconds, to release their aromatic oils.

STAGE 2: onions

The base of most curries, so getting them right is crucial. Always make sure they are cooked through until soft and turning golden at the edges. After that, the further you cook them the deeper the flavours of the curry. For a lamb or chicken curry, cook onions until the edges are well-browned. In curries containing more delicate ingredients - such as vegetables or some seafood - onions only need to be golden, or their resonant taste could overpower the rest of the dish.

STAGE 3: garlic and ginger

I often make a paste of ginger and garlic for a smoother sauce. For small amounts, I grate both on a Microplane. For larger quantities, chop them coarsely, use a small stick blender and add a little water to help break them down. Cooking garlic fully is essential. You can tell when it's cooked by the fragrance, which changes from raw and strong to mellow. In a paste, garlic will start to look grainy and turn a pale gold colour.

STAGE 4: ground spices

grinding Whether you use a mortar and pestle, a spice grinder or a clean coffee grinder, make sure spices are really well ground so they melt into the sauce. Any gritty spices added will remain so in the finished dish.
cooking These burn easily so keep the heat down and stir often. Many people add a little water with their spices to ensure they don't scorch. They will cook in 40 seconds, or two minutes if you add water.

STAGE 5: tomatoes and/or yogurt

tomatoes Once these have been added, the ingredients in the pot are thought of as a 'masala', which simply means the mixed and spiced base of a sauce. The masala lets you know when it is cooked by releasing some oil back into the pan, so look for droplets of oil on the base as you stir. If you're not sure if a masala is ready, try a little. It should taste smooth. If it's still too strong, add some water and cook it for a little longer. Once the masala is cooked, you can *bhuno* it (see right).

yogurt This adds sourness and creaminess. You have to be careful, as it can split in the pan; this isn't a disaster but will mean the dish isn't as creamy as it could be. To avoid curdling, use full-fat yogurt at room temperature, as the fat stabilises the yogurt and a cold product added to a hot pan is more likely to split. Add yogurt in batches if it is a large quantity, stir constantly until it comes to a boil and continue to do so for a further few minutes. It should now be fine with only an occasional stir.

slow-cooking

In the early days of Indian restaurants in Britain, a curry was left on very low heat for hours with a chef stirring it every time he passed. This helped the flavours fully develop and, with every stir, the ingredients broke down into a more homogenous sauce. When you have time, try cooking your curry more slowly than the recipe suggests, stirring often, to help the ingredients melt together.

the bhuno-ing process

In Indian cookery dishes are often 'bhunoed', or browned, towards the end, to intensify the flavours, while constant stirring improves the consistency of the sauce. To bhuno a recipe, increase the heat and stir constantly for four to six minutes as the sauce reduces. If your pan seems dry, add a splash of water and bhuno until reduced again.

the role of water

When you start to cook, put the kettle on. You'll need to add water while cooking a curry and, if it's cold, you'll bring the temperature down in the pan, prolonging the cooking time and - some say - affecting the taste. Add a little at any time if you think an ingredient's about to burn before it's properly cooked, then cook off excess before moving to the next stage. Though I indicate specific quantities, be aware of how much liquid is in the pan; your heat may be higher than mine, or your pot wider with more chance for water to evaporate off.

a bony issue

I keep bones in fish, poultry and meat; it adds so much flavour. Indians cook fish steaks, heads and tails in a curry for maximum taste, while poultry and meat are cut into small bone-in pieces. But many people hate bones. If you want to use fish fillets, ask your fishmonger for a firm white fish that won't flake too easily. Halibut is great. And if you really hate eating meat off the bone, ask your butcher for some bones to add to the pot while cooking, which can easily be removed before serving.

balancing the final dish

Just as a chef should never let a single dish leave his kitchen without tasting it, you must taste your curry at the end of cooking and before serving. A curry is a delicate balance of sweet, sour, spicy and salty and you need to correct all these flavours to achieve the most delicious dish. Here are your most important tools.

a note about chillies In all my recipes, I suggest a variable amount of chillies (such as 1-3) you could add. I want to leave it up to you to balance the heat of a dish to suit yourself. But, when using dried chillies, you should usually shake out and discard the seeds before preparing them, or your dish will be too hot.

add heat… Sprinkle in chilli flakes or halve a green chilli lengthways, add to the pot and simmer for few minutes.

…or tame the flame Add a little cream, coconut cream or sugar, depending on the other ingredients in the curry.

to add sweetness Use a little sugar, cream or coconut cream, depending on the dish. Restaurants add caramelised onion paste: to do the same, fry onions until golden or brown, depending on the dish (remembering delicate curries will be overwhelmed by over-brown onions), then blend with a little water until smooth.

for more acidity Try lemon juice, tamarind paste, dried mango or pomegranate powder, even sour cream. Be guided by the other ingredients in the curry as to which souring agent is most suitable.

to perk things up Add garam masala for warming spices, cumin powder (raw or roasted, see page 55) for earthy depth and black pepper for aromatic heat.

sleep on it Many curries improve overnight, as the flavours mature and permeate the main ingredients. You can cook chicken, meat, potato and lentil curries a day earlier, they will taste even better tomorrow.

serving a brilliant Indian meal

You can relax; there are no 'rules' about how to serve curry. Even traditional Indian dining mores were as fragmented as the country itself and every region - even every family - had its own customs.

In our Punjabi home we ate one-course meals with either rice or flatbreads, not both. Pickles were only brought out when the meal was very simple, and chutneys only served with snacks. At the other end of the spectrum, Bengali meals had a succession of courses, each dish eaten only with rice. Yet again, my husband's Marwari family ate three courses, the first something sweet, then flatbreads with vegetables and raita, then rice with lentils or a yogurt curry. They finished with poppadoms, used to cleanse the palate.

As India has evolved, all such dining norms have been further diluted. The modern generation have their own rules, based loosely on how they grew up, but tailored to suit their lifestyles. As is the case all around the world, time is now at a premium, so dishes will be simplified, though the meal will remain well balanced, containing protein, carbohydrates and - if possible - fresh seasonal vegetables, even in the poorest families. These days we cook to the beat of our own drum, even if that drum has on it a faded (in my case), Made in Punjab stamp.

entertaining the indian way
When Indian people entertain, it is with huge generosity of spirit. Guests are always served the best food their hosts can afford. Punjabis are known for their love of food and people, and my childhood had an abundance of both. My parents entertained large groups of people regularly and my mother always made enough to feed her guests twice over!

The evening would start with drinks and appetisers which were bite-sized pieces of heaven: kebabs, mini samosas, crisp little potato cakes and more, all served with our family's spicy Tangy Herb Chutney (see page 27). As a girl I would have helped my mother in the kitchen earlier in the day, carefully filling samosas or shaping tiny potato cakes. These wonderful appetisers were the inspiration for my exciting and tempting 'bites', and the recipes for them start overleaf!

When we got to the table, there would be three or four curries, two of them always vegetarian, containing lentils or paneer. There would follow an array of vegetable sides, all carefully chosen for their different colours and textures, breads, rice and raita. There was always an Indian dessert, but also fresh or cooked fruits.

entertaining my way...
I have inherited my mother's entertaining style but have adapted it to be a little simpler and more practical for a modern way of life. My parties are smaller - and I have less time than my mother did - but my menu will still have a wonderful variety of vibrant colours, textures and flavours. There will always be rice and warm breads (some bought in, to achieve a good broad selection) and pickles... if I remember! I make only one appetiser, but often also provide a dip with crunchy crudités and some spiced nuts (see page 26). I like fruity desserts after Indian meals, to refresh the palate.

... and your way
Everyone has their own style and you must be true to your own. Don't overextend yourself with a complicated menu; it will just cause stress, which is not the point of having people over. Serve just one great curry, a vegetable or two, a raita and some rice or naan. That's more than enough to make your guests feel special and enjoy a great evening. The good news is that most curries improve overnight (though I would advise making those with vegetables, fish and seafood on the day of serving). Even a pilaf reheats really well in the microwave, covered with damp kitchen paper, while breads and dessert can be bought in. Entertaining should be a pleasure. It is about showing love for your friends, having a good time and living life according to your own rules.

1 BITES

chicken kathi rolls

One of my favourite starters: delicious chicken, a tangle of onions, tomatoes and herb chutney all wrapped in lovely pastry. I have been eating variations of this dish since childhood. You can substitute the chicken for lamb or even Fresh Paneer (see page 25) or stir-fried chickpeas. It does have a few stages, but is really easy to do and all the components can be prepared earlier in the day. I use puff pastry here, as it has the same character as the traditional paratha and is easily available, but make it with Paratha (see page 157) if you prefer.

Whizz together all the ingredients for the marinade with 2 tbsp water until smooth. Place the chicken in the marinade and leave for as long as possible (a minimum of one hour, or up to overnight in the fridge).

Using a 10cm bowl or saucer as a guide, cut out five circles from the pastry. Take one at a time and roll each out into thinner 15cm circles, using a little flour to help. Heat a non-stick frying pan, place in a pastry round, and cook until golden spots appear on the base (around 20 seconds), then turn over and cook the other side until golden. Meanwhile, spread a good layer of the egg over the upper surface, using a small spoon. Then flip and cook the egg side for 10 seconds. Take out and place on a plate. Repeat with the others.

Heat a saucepan, add the chicken and marinade and stir-fry for two or three minutes, or until you can see droplets of oil on the base of the pan. Add a splash of water (to deglaze the base) and the onion and cook for another minute or so until the chicken is done. Add the tomato, stir for 20 seconds, then remove from the heat. Taste and adjust the seasoning.

Taking one 'bread' at a time, egg side up, spoon a line of the chicken mixture down the centre, then add a rounded tablespoon of the chutney. Roll into a log and slice in half.

You can make these ahead, wrap the finished rolls in foil and reheat in the oven when you are ready to serve, but they will be a little softer.

makes 10 pieces

for the marinade
15g fresh root ginger, peeled weight
4 fat garlic cloves
2½ tbsp lemon juice
1½ tsp ground cumin
2 tbsp vegetable oil
¾–1 tsp chilli powder
¾ tsp garam masala
salt, to taste
¼ tsp freshly ground black pepper

for the rolls
2 chicken breasts (around 160g each), cut into small cubes
400g packet ready-rolled puff pastry
plain flour, to dust
2 small eggs, beaten
1 onion, sliced
1 large vine tomato, sliced into strips
1 x recipe Tangy Herb Chutney (see page 27)

mixed vegetable pakoras

These delicious north Indian snacks are loved by everyone. They are really quick to make, so are great when you have unexpected guests. In India they love to eat hot pakoras in the monsoon season, when it is wet and rainy and they are stuck indoors. You can use any vegetable you like as long as it is not watery. We generally use a selection, but you can use just one type. Serve with Tangy Herb Chutney (see page 27).

Whisk together all the ingredients for the batter with 150ml water. Taste and adjust the seasoning; it should be slightly overseasoned. If using onions among your vegetables, salt them now and leave for a short while until they start to wilt, then rinse and pat dry.

Heat 7.5cm of oil in a large, wide saucepan, karahi or wok. It should be around 180°C or, if you don't have a thermometer, a drop of batter should start sizzling immediately.

Cook one type of vegetable at a time, finishing with the onions. Dip the pieces of potato, cauliflower or aubergine in the batter, then drop them into the pan in batches, making sure not to crowd the pan.

Reduce the heat so the vegetables cook as the batter browns. Once they are done, remove from the pan with a slotted spoon and place on a plate lined with kitchen paper.

Throw the wilted onions in the remaining batter, then take a small walnut-sized ball of them at a time and add it to the pan. Once they are golden brown, remove with a slotted spoon and drain on kitchen paper.

Serve each batch hot as you cook the next.

serves 4–6

for the batter
100g gram flour
2 tsp ground rice (optional, but it makes them crispy)
1 good tsp salt, or to taste
⅔ tsp carom seeds (if you have them)
½–¾ tsp chilli powder
½ tsp turmeric
2 tsp ground coriander
1½ tsp ground cumin
⅔ tsp garam masala
1½ tsp dried mango powder
2 garlic cloves, grated into a paste

for the vegetables
1 small onion, sliced
vegetable oil, to deep-fry
100g potato, peeled and sliced 1cm thick
150g cauliflower or broccoli, cut into small-medium florets
100g aubergines, cut into 1cm slices or half moons

spicy prawn cakes

These Goan-inspired cakes are delicious and moreish; perfect as canapés. You can buy finely grated frozen coconut in many Asian supermarkets; keep it in the freezer and defrost the amount you need. If you can't find any, use unsweetened desiccated coconut. These prawn cakes are delicious simply with a squeeze of lime or lemon, or with Tangy Herb Chutney (see page 27). If you choose the chutney, try adding a couple of spoons of coconut to the recipe, then adjust the tartness.

Using a sturdy mortar and pestle, pound the whole spices to a powder.

Heat half the oil in a small non-stick saucepan and fry the onion until softened and turning golden at the edges. Add the ginger and garlic and cook on a gentle flame for a couple of minutes, or until the garlic is cooked. Add the salt and all the spices and cook, stirring, for another 20 seconds. Add the prawns and stir-fry until cooked (around two minutes).

Tip everything from the pan into a blender with the crumbs and coconut and roughly blend to a coarse paste; a few larger pieces of prawn left in the mix is ideal. Taste and adjust the seasoning and chilli, then stir in the egg and the chopped coriander. Set aside and allow to rest for 10 minutes.

Heat the remaining oil in a large non-stick frying pan. Make small balls from the mixture and pat into 5cm cakes. Shallow-fry gently for two or three minutes each side, until golden, crisp and heated through to the centre. You will need to do this in two batches.

Serve with lime or lemon wedges or Tangy Herb Chutney (see page 27).

makes 20 small cakes

4 cloves
2.5cm cinnamon stick
10 black peppercorns
5 tbsp vegetable oil
1 onion, finely chopped
16g fresh root ginger, peeled weight, chopped
4 fat garlic cloves, chopped
salt, to taste
1½ tsp ground cumin
¾-1¼ tsp chilli powder, or to taste
400g small-to-medium raw prawns, shelled, deveined and rinsed
4 large slices white bread, crusts removed, made into crumbs
80g finely grated frozen coconut, or 4 tbsp unsweetened desiccated coconut
2 eggs, beaten
large handful of chopped fresh coriander

salmon tikka lettuce wraps

I think salmon works really well in tandoori-style dishes and this 'fusion food' starter is as stunning in colour as it is in taste. The earthy tandoori salmon is lifted by the creamy herb dressing and tart capers. The red cabbage has a lovely mustardy flavour but is mostly there for a colour contrast, so I leave it to you to decide whether to add it or not.

Mix together the ingredients for the marinade until smooth. Season well and taste; it should be slightly overseasoned at this point. Add the salmon, turn to coat and marinate for one hour.

Meanwhile, mix together the ingredients for the topping and season with salt and lots of freshly ground pepper.

When you are ready to serve, preheat your grill to high (I use the grill setting in my oven and place the baking tray on the top shelf). Place the fish on a baking tray lined with greaseproof paper or foil and grill for seven to nine minutes, turning once, or until the fish is just done and charring in places.

Meanwhile, lay out the lettuce leaves. When the fish is done, cut each fillet lengthwise into four or five pieces, then break up into large chunks. Place each broken-up piece into a lettuce leaf. Add a teaspoon of the topping and scatter with a few capers. Sprinkle with the cabbage (if using) and serve immediately.

makes 8–10, can be doubled

for the tandoori marinade
50g plain yogurt
6g fresh root ginger, peeled weight, grated into a paste
2 garlic cloves, grated into a paste
2 tsp gram flour
1 tsp paprika
¾ tsp chilli powder
1½ tbsp vegetable oil
¾ tsp ground cumin
¼ tsp freshly ground black pepper
1 tbsp lemon juice
1 tbsp light crème fraîche

for the wraps
2 small, skinless salmon fillets
8–10 even-sized Baby Gem lettuce leaves, washed and dried
2 tbsp capers
a little finely shredded red cabbage (optional)

for the topping
30g Greek yogurt
30g light crème fraîche
10g finely chopped onion
10g finely chopped fresh coriander
1–2 green chillies, deseeded and finely chopped (optional)
salt, to taste

crispy chilli squid

I love this way of cooking squid, perhaps because I have so many fond memories of eating calamari under the Mediterranean sun, or maybe it's the texture of the soft squid against the crisp coating. The marinade adds a kick while the lovely mayonnaise finishes it off and is especially good at flattering squid which hasn't had enough time in the marinade. But you can forget the mayonnaise and serve the squid simply with lemon wedges, if you prefer.

Whizz together all the ingredients for the marinade with 2 tbsp water to make a fine paste. Mix into the squid and leave to marinate for an hour or more, or for several hours in the fridge.

Stir together the ingredients for the mayonnaise and season to taste.

Heat around 7.5cm of vegetable oil in a wok, karahi or saucepan until a small piece of bread dropped in sizzles immediately.

Mix together the semolina and flour. Remove the squid from its marinade and dredge it in the flour mixture. Pat off any excess, then add the squid to the deep-frying pan in two or three batches (make sure not to overcrowd the pan). Fry for two to three minutes, or until golden and crisp.

Remove with a slotted spoon, place on kitchen paper and keep warm while you fry the remaining squid. Serve hot, with the mayonnaise on the side.

serves 4

for the marinade
2 fresh large fat red chillies, deseeded
10g fresh root ginger, peeled weight
3 large garlic cloves
1½ tbsp white wine vinegar
1½ tbsp vegetable oil
¾ tsp ground cumin
salt, to taste

for the squid
300g prepared squid, rings, tentacles and flaps
vegetable oil, for deep-frying
3 tbsp semolina
5 tbsp plain flour

for the chilli, lemon and garlic mayonnaise
150g mayonnaise (the better the quality, the less sweet)
3 tsp lemon juice
freshly ground black pepper, to taste
1 tsp chilli powder, or to taste
1 fat garlic clove, grated into a paste, or to taste

lamb kebabs with mint and cucumber dip

I like to serve these kebabs piled on a platter with a bowl of the dip and some soft flatbreads (flour tortillas or Indian breads) and toothpicks on the side. Then some people can tear off some bread and use it to scoop up a piece of lamb and yogurt, while others can skewer the lamb with a toothpick and dip it in the thick, luscious dip; others still will just eat the bread with the dip. You can also serve the lamb with Tangy Herb Chutney (see page 27) for a more traditional take.

Blend together the ingredients for the marinade until smooth. Taste and make sure it is over-seasoned, as the lamb will need it. Add the lamb and leave for as long as possible (overnight in the fridge is best). Bring back to room temperature before continuing.

Grate the cucumber coarsely, then squeeze out all the excess water, using your fists or a tea towel to help. Add to the yogurt along with the remaining dip ingredients.

Heat the grill to a high setting. Place the lamb on a baking tray lined with foil and grill for six to eight minutes, turning halfway, or until done to your liking. Sprinkle with the chaat masala (if using).

Serve hot with the cool cucumber and mint dip and flatbreads (see recipe introduction).

serves 6

for the marinade
15g fresh root ginger, peeled weight, grated into a paste
5 fat garlic cloves, grated into a paste
4 tbsp Greek yogurt
3 tbsp vegetable oil
2 tsp garam masala
2 tsp ground cumin
$\frac{2}{3}$ tsp black pepper
1 tsp chilli powder
2½ tbsp lemon juice
salt, to taste

for the lamb
400-450g leg of lamb, in 2.5cm cubes
1 tsp chaat masala (optional)

for the mint and cucumber dip
150g cucumber
200g Greek yogurt
1 tbsp tahini paste
15 large mint leaves, shredded
1 green chilli, deseeded and finely chopped (optional)
1½ tbsp olive oil
$\frac{1}{3}$ tsp freshly ground black pepper

quick steamed pea cakes

These light, fluffy cakes are a fantastic starter or teatime snack. I serve them with Tangy Herb Chutney (see page 27) but they taste lovely just as they are. There are special deep-sided steel plates or tins which are used in India for this type of steamed cake, but I use two small 15cm baking tins in a double steamer. If you don't have a steamer, boil water in a wide pan, place a pudding bowl filled with water inside and place the tin on top. (If you do this, don't use a springform tin, or the water will rise up into the batter.) If you don't have a double steamer and need to make the recipe in two batches, make the batter up to the point of adding the baking powder and bicarbonate of soda, then halve it. Then add half the raising agents to half the batter, cook, and repeat with the remaining batter.

Oil two 15cm steel plates with deep sides, or baking tins. Pour about 7.5cm water into the base of a double steamer or a wide and deep saucepan (see recipe introduction). Cover and bring to a boil.

Meanwhile, blend the peas, lemon juice, oil, ginger and chillies to a smooth paste with 120ml water. Stir in the gram flour and salt. Taste to check the seasoning. Stir in the baking powder and bicarbonate of soda and divide between the oiled tins. Carefully place them in the steamer, cover and steam on a moderate to high heat for 18 minutes, or until a toothpick inserted into the centre comes out clean.

Remove from the steamer and leave to cool for 10 minutes, then run a knife around the edge of the tins and turn the pea cakes out on to a plate.

Heat the oil for the tarka in a small pan and add the mustard seeds. When they are popping well, add the sesame seeds and, once they start to colour, the curry leaves. Stir for five seconds, then spoon evenly over the cakes. Cut the cakes into diamonds, squares or wedges. Serve hot or at room temperature.

serves 4–6, can be halved

for the pea cakes
2 tbsp vegetable oil, plus more for the tins
170g frozen peas, defrosted
5 tbsp lemon juice
16g fresh root ginger, peeled weight, roughly quartered
2–4 green chillies (ideally Indian finger), stalk removed
140g gram flour
salt, to taste
$2/3$ tsp baking powder
$2/3$ tsp bicarbonate of soda

for the tarka
4 tsp vegetable oil
1 tsp mustard seeds
2 tsp sesame seeds
16 fresh curry leaves

paneer bruschetta

I love bruschetta in the summer and make my Indian version with fresh paneer, which has the creaminess of mozzarella but a different texture. It is easy to make, fresh, vibrant and lovely for a light lunch with salad, or as a pre-dinner appetiser. Do not use store-bought paneer; it can be rubbery and would ruin the freshness of this bruschetta. Paneer is really easy to make and with very few ingredients; you can also make it a day ahead and keep it in the fridge, covered with damp muslin or kitchen paper. Normally, paneer is set into a hard block, but here I only press it for 15–20 minutes for a softer texture. I use ciabatta, but you can use any good-quality bread.

1 x recipe Fresh Paneer (see below)
3 tbsp finely chopped onion, or to taste
2 green chillies (ideally Indian green finger), finely sliced
large handful of finely chopped fresh coriander, leaves and stalks
150g baby plum tomatoes, chopped
2 big tbsp good-quality olive oil
¼ tsp coarsely ground black pepper
salt, to taste
1 ciabatta or other good-quality loaf, sliced into 1½cm slices on the diagonal

Crumble the paneer into a bowl in smallish chunks. Add the onion, chillies, coriander, tomatoes, olive oil and black pepper and season to taste with salt. Stir well and allow to sit until you are ready to eat.

Just before eating, toast or griddle the bread, spoon the mixture on top and serve.

makes 8–9 pieces, can be doubled

fresh paneer

Bring the milk to a boil in a heavy-based saucepan. Once the milk starts to rise up in the pan, stir in the lemon juice. Keep stirring until the milk splits, adding more lemon if it doesn't; the curds will eventually separate from the watery whey. Remove from the heat and pour into a muslin-lined sieve to drain off the water. Rinse the paneer in cold water. Make a little bundle of the paneer in the muslin, twist the open ends of the muslin together to form a round cheese, place on a work top and top with a heavy weight (I use a saucepan filled with water). Leave for 15 minutes (I put it in or near my sink, so the curds can drain away down the plug hole), then remove the weight. Use immediately, or cover with damp muslin or kitchen paper and keep in the fridge for a day.

1 litre whole milk
3 tbsp lemon juice, plus more if needed

makes 160g

quick spiced cashew nuts

You can buy lots of spiced nuts in the shops these days, but making them at home is really quick and easy and you can spice them to taste.

Melt the butter in a frying pan. Add the cashew nuts and sauté until lightly roasted. Turn off the heat and stir in all the remaining ingredients. Pour into a bowl and leave to cool.

makes enough for 5–6

1 rounded tsp butter
200g raw, unsalted cashew nuts
½ tsp salt
½ tsp freshly ground black pepper
¼–½ tsp chilli powder
1 tsp ground cumin
½ tsp dried mango powder

creamy mint chutney

This is that lovely, refreshing dip that is often on the table as you start your curry house meal. I always find that I pick at it to start with, then keep it to eat with tandoori food. It is a lovely, sweet, spicy and lightly sour chutney that goes really well with all grills, barbecues and many snacks. I prefer to use measurements such as 'a small handful' for tiny amounts of herbs; however mint can be very strong, so it's best to measure it out for this recipe, so as not to overpower the dish.

Blend all the ingredients together until smooth. Taste, adjust the seasoning, adding more tamarind paste or lemon if you want more tang, then serve.

serves 4–6

7g mint leaves, washed
20g fresh coriander leaves and stalks, washed
1–2 green chillies (preferably Indian green finger), stalk removed
2 tsp sugar
½ tsp tamarind paste, or to taste
1 tsp lemon juice, or to taste
150g plain yogurt
⅓ tsp roasted cumin powder (see page 55)

tangy herb chutney

An incredibly versatile recipe, this is the cornerstone of all north Indian snacks. We love it with our samosas, bhajis, pakoras, kebabs… and most other things! There are many variations, some people will add a little sugar, some raw garlic and others yogurt. This is how we like it in my family and it is a perfect base from which to experiment.

60g fresh coriander, leaves and stalks
2½ tbsp lemon juice
2 green chillies, deseeded if you prefer
12g mint leaves
20g raw or roasted unsalted pistachios
salt, to taste

Blend together all the ingredients with 4 tbsp water until smooth; it might take a few minutes. Taste and adjust the seasoning. Keep in a glass jar in the fridge for up to a week, or freeze until ready to use.

makes around 200ml

fresh mango chutney

The typical mango chutneys you find in Indian restaurants are made from unripe green mangoes but, as these are hard to find, I decided to come up with my own recipe for a fresh mango chutney. It is delicious, spicy and fruity.

2 tsp vegetable oil
2–5 dried red chillies, or to taste
1 tsp cumin seeds
1 tsp fennel seeds
180ml white wine vinegar
40–50g sugar (depends on the sweetness of the mangoes)
salt and a little black pepper, to taste
2 large ripe mangoes, peeled, stoned and cut into pieces (see page 169)

Heat the oil in a saucepan and add the whole chillies, cumin and fennel seeds. Once the cumin is aromatic (a matter of seconds) and the chillies are darker, add the vinegar, sugar, 160ml water and a little salt and pepper. Simmer for six or seven minutes. Add the mango and cook for six or seven minutes more, or until the mango is soft and easy to mash.

Mash half the mango pieces into the chutney and mix well. It should be thick, but not jammy. Serve hot or cold.

makes one largish bowl

puchkas

These are little taste bombs and I don't know anyone who doesn't love them. Small, crisp, hollow balls of semolina pastry are filled with potatoes, chickpeas, yogurt, then both a sweet-and-sour and a herb chutney. They are topped with sev, which look like fine yellow pieces of thread. You place the puchkas in your mouth whole and bite into an explosion of tastes and textures. Buy the tamarind chutney if you don't want to make the quick recipe here, and pani puris and sev are available in Indian shops (look for the handmade variety). This looks complicated, but is really easy and indescribably delicious.

For the tamarind chutney, place the tamarind, sugar and 6 tbsp water in a small saucepan. Bring to a boil and simmer for three minutes. Add the salt, pepper and ¾ tsp of roasted cumin powder (reserve the rest) and cook until the chutney is syrupy (another minute or two). You should have around 4 tbsp of chutney. If it becomes hard as it sits, loosen it with 1 tbsp boiling water.

Whisk the yogurt with a little salt, the chilli powder and reserved roasted cumin powder until smooth. Set aside.

Boil the potato in salted water until tender, then peel and cut into 1cm cubes.

Assemble the puchkas when you are ready to eat. You will find that the puris have a thicker, harder side and a thinner side… it might not be so obvious at first, but when you tap both convex sides with your fingernail you will easily spot the thinner side. Break a 2.5cm hole in the thinner side with your finger. Fill each puri with a couple of chickpeas and a piece of potato. Spoon 1 tsp yogurt into each and top with ⅓ tsp each of tamarind chutney and Tangy Herb Chutney. Sprinkle generously with the sev (if using) and serve immediately.

makes 20, enough for 4–5 people

for the quick sweet-and-sour tamarind chutney
2 good tsp tamarind paste
35–40g jaggery, chopped up, or 3¾ tbsp sugar
¼ tsp salt
¼–⅓ tsp freshly ground black pepper
1 rounded tsp roasted cumin powder (see page 55)

for the puchkas
200g plain yogurt, not too sour
salt, to taste
scant ¼ tsp chilli powder
100g potato
20 ready-made puris (sold as pani puris)
50g cooked chickpeas, rinsed
½ x recipe Tangy Herb Chutney, (see page 27)
handful of sev (optional)

2 THE CURRIES

vegetable

velvety black lentil curry

This is essentially the restaurant-style lentil dish that we all love. A professional kitchen would leave these cooking really gently overnight on top of the warm tandoor oven so they turn into an even, creamy mass. Don't worry, you don't have to do the same! This curry is in fact very simple to make, though it takes a while to cook, and the flavour of earthy lentils, tart tomatoes, spices, rich cream and butter is divine. Serve with Naan (see page 155) or Paratha (see page 157).

Wash the black gram and pick out and discard any discoloured lentils you can see. Place them in a large bowl, cover with fresh water and leave to soak for at least two hours, or preferably overnight.

Rinse the lentils and tip them, with 1½ litres of fresh water, into a large saucepan. Bring to a boil, then reduce the heat, cover and simmer gently for 1–1½ hours, or until soft; stir occasionally and top up with water, if necessary.

Meanwhile, blend together the 20g ginger, garlic and tomatoes until smooth (I use my trusty stick blender). Pour this mixture into the soft lentils along with some salt, cover and cook for a further hour. Stir occasionally and add extra hot water, if necessary.

By now the lentils should be very soft and a little creamy. Lightly mash some of them against the side of the pan with your spoon. Add the cream, butter, spices, crushed fenugreek leaves and a little more salt, to taste, along with the red kidney beans. Cook for another 10 minutes, mashing a few more of the lentils if necessary until you have a creamy, homogenous curry. Taste, adjust the seasoning and sprinkle with the ginger julienne.

serves 4

80g whole black gram
20g fresh root ginger, peeled weight, plus a little in julienne to serve
5 large garlic cloves
4 largish tomatoes
salt, to taste
80–100ml double cream
2–4 tbsp butter, or to taste
¼–½ tsp chilli powder, or to taste
¾ tsp ground cumin
1 tsp garam masala, or to taste
¾ tsp dried fenugreek leaves, crushed
100g cooked red kidney beans

spinach with black-eyed peas

A simple, everyday main course that shows how most Indians eat: a no-fuss dish with fresh vegetables and some sort of protein. This is only lightly spiced, so as not to overpower the spinach, and goes well with rice, breads and a little yogurt.

Heat the oil in a non-stick saucepan. Add the mustard and fenugreek seeds and whole dried chillies. Once the mustard seeds have spluttered, add the garlic and curry leaves and cook them gently until the garlic is just starting to turn golden.

Add the spinach, seasoning and a splash of water; mix well and cover. Cook for five to seven minutes, until well wilted, stirring occasionally. Add the ground coriander and cumin, half the black-eyed peas and a splash of water. Cover and cook for five or six minutes. Take out one-third of the mix and blend to a fine puree. Return to the pan with the remaining beans.

Stir in the tamarind paste and peanuts. Boil off any excess water: you should be left with a slightly thick, creamy mass. Taste and adjust the seasoning and tartness, adding more tamarind if you would like more tang, and serve.

serves 4

3 tbsp vegetable oil
rounded ½ tsp mustard seeds
½ tsp fenugreek seeds
2–4 dried red chillies
5 garlic cloves, finely chopped or
   grated into a paste
14 fresh curry leaves
250g whole leaf spinach, shredded,
   or baby spinach, washed well
salt, to taste
lots of freshly ground black pepper
1 tsp ground coriander
1 rounded tsp ground cumin
400g can of black-eyed peas, drained
   well and rinsed
1½–2 tsp tamarind paste, or to taste
good handful of roasted and salted
   peanuts

creamy almond vegetable curry

The yogurt and toasted almonds give this a wonderful nutty flavour, while the vegetables remain vibrant. I blanch and toast my own almonds, but you can buy them blanched and ready-toasted if this is a step too far. Use whatever non-watery vegetables you like, or different nuts. I blanch my vegetables and finish them in the gravy so they don't lose their character, but you can add them straight into the bubbling curry if you prefer, or even sauté them in butter first. Serve with Naan (see page 155), Paratha (see page 157), or a pilaf (see pages 160-163).

Heat 1 tsp oil in a small pan and fry the almonds until well and evenly golden. Pour them straight into a mortar and crush to a powder with the pestle.

Heat the remaining oil in a large non-stick saucepan and add the cloves, cardamom and caraway seeds. Follow after 20 seconds with the onion and cook until golden on the edges. Scrape in the ginger and garlic pastes and sauté gently for one or two minutes, or until the garlic is just golden.

Add the ground spices and yogurt and bring to a boil, stirring constantly. Continue to cook until the oil leaves the masala. It should take five to eight minutes. Add 250ml water and bring to a boil, then simmer gently for 10–12 minutes more.

Cook your vegetables as you like them (see recipe introduction). To blanch mine, I bring a pot of salted water to a boil as the sauce is cooking and add my potatoes. After five minutes I add the carrots. Once they are cooked, I fish them out and add my broccoli and, three minutes later, the mangetout and peas. I drain them after another minute or so.

Now add the vegetables, salt, cream, tomatoes and crushed almonds, then cook for another two or three minutes for everything to come together. The sauce should be thick, creamy and slightly granular from the nuts. Add a small splash of water, if necessary. Check the seasoning and serve.

serves 3–4

to blanch almonds Place whole almonds in a small bowl, cover with boiling water and leave for 30 minutes or so. The skins will loosen and wrinkle. Peel them off the nuts to reveal creamy, blanched almonds.

for the curry
4 tbsp vegetable oil, plus 1 tsp
60g blanched almonds
6 cloves
6 green cardamom pods
1 tsp caraway seeds
1 smallish onion, finely chopped
15g fresh root ginger, peeled weight, grated into a paste
4 fat garlic cloves, grated into a paste
1⅓ tsp ground cumin
2 tsp ground coriander
¼ tsp turmeric
⅛–¼ tsp chilli powder, or to taste
4 tbsp plain yogurt
salt, to taste
6 tbsp single cream
8 cherry tomatoes, halved

for the vegetables
125g potatoes, peeled and cut into 2cm cubes
60g carrots, peeled and cut into half moons
70g broccoli, cut into small florets
60g mangetout, trimmed
large handful of peas

everyday lentil and vegetable curry

A staple for many people on the west coast of India. There are many variations; some are hotter, others add ginger or garlic. I like to make it with the added vegetables here, so I don't need to cook another dish. You can adapt this nearly endlessly to your tastes, with or without the sugar, coconut and vegetables. Choose any vegetables you like, though starchy varieties aren't traditional. I have listed those I often use, but I vary them depending on the season and what I have in the fridge.

Put the lentils in a big pan with 1 litre of water and bring to a boil. If any scum forms on top, skim it off. Add the turmeric. Reduce the heat and simmer until the lentils are really soft and starting to break down; it should take around 20 minutes. Add the aubergines (if using) and continue cooking gently.

Meanwhile, make the tarka. Heat the oil in a small saucepan. Add the mustard, cumin and sesame seeds, split black lentils (if using), cloves and whole dried chillies. Once the mustard seeds have stopped popping, add the curry leaves and, a beat later, the onions. Cook gently until the onions are soft and starting to colour. Add the tomatoes, okra (if using), ground coriander and salt. Stir-fry for four minutes and, once the tomatoes start to soften, pour everything into the lentil curry. Add the tamarind, coconut and sugar (if using). Add the green beans (if using) and simmer for five minutes, or until your vegetables are done. Taste, adjust the salt, sugar and tamarind, then serve.

serves 4–5

for the curry
200g split pigeon pea lentils (*tovar dal*), well washed
⅓ tsp turmeric
1 tsp tamarind paste, or to taste
2 tbsp unsweetened desiccated coconut (optional)
1½–2½ tsp sugar, or to taste (optional)

for the tarka
2 tbsp vegetable oil
1 tsp mustard seeds
1 tsp cumin seeds
1 tsp sesame seeds (optional)
2 tsp split and husked black gram (*urad dal*), if you have it
2 cloves
2–3 dried red chillies
12 fresh curry leaves
2 small onions, finely sliced
2 tomatoes, each cut into 6 wedges
1½ tsp ground coriander
salt, to taste

for the vegetables (optional)
3 Japanese or small aubergines, halved lengthwise then cut across into 3
8 okra, topped, tailed and halved widthways
handful of green beans

karahi mushrooms with peppers and peas

A lovely vegetarian dish that manages to be both hearty and delicate at the same time. It can serve two as a main dish, or up to four if it is to accompany other things. I like to use a selection of mushrooms, as they all add their own flavour and texture to the dish. Don't use portabella mushrooms, though, as they make the whole thing turn black. I use equal quantities of oyster, shiitake and chestnut mushrooms. Leave the oyster mushrooms whole, or tear them in half if they are large.

4 tbsp vegetable oil
250g mushrooms, cleaned, in 2cm
  slices (see recipe introduction)
salt, to taste
½ tsp coriander seeds, lightly crushed
1 small onion, finely chopped
6g fresh root ginger, peeled weight,
  grated into a paste
3 garlic cloves, grated into a paste
3 tomatoes, blended to a puree with
  a stick blender
1 tsp ground coriander
¾ tsp ground cumin
¾–1 tsp garam masala
⅛ tsp chilli powder, or to taste
¾ large red pepper, in coarse dice
generous handful of green peas
2 tbsp double cream (optional)
small handful of chopped fresh
  coriander leaves, to serve

Heat half the oil in a large non-stick sauté pan or karahi. Add the mushrooms and a little salt and sauté over a moderate flame for four to five minutes, until they have a lovely golden tinge. Remove from the pan and set aside.

Heat the remaining oil, add the coriander seeds and, once they have darkened a little, the onion. Cook until golden. Add the ginger and garlic pastes and cook, stirring, over a low flame for one to two minutes, or until you can smell that the garlic is cooked. Pour in the tomatoes and add the remaining spices. Season and cook, stirring occasionally, for eight to 10 minutes, or until the paste releases some oil back into the pan.

Stir in the pepper dice, peas and a good splash of water, cover and cook for four minutes, or until the peppers are softening. Add the mushrooms, cover and allow the flavours to come together for a few minutes. Stir in the cream (if using) and about 50ml water, or enough to form a light sauce. Bring to a boil, taste, adjust the seasoning and sprinkle with the chopped coriander.

serves 4

tarka dhal

This is a classic, it is absolutely wonderful and easy to make. Tarka simply means a few ingredients fried up and stirred in at the end; most Indian lentil dishes are made this way. Many restaurant tarka dhals often have two tarkas; the first prepared as in this recipe and the second as fried cumin seeds and sliced garlic poured over the top. I haven't done the latter as I didn't want to add another step and all the flavour you need is already here. But feel free to fry two or three finely sliced garlic cloves or a small onion in lots of oil until golden (garlic) or well-browned and slightly crisp (onions), then pile them on top.

Wash both types of lentils together in several changes of water. Place the lentils and 1 litre of water in a large saucepan. Bring to a boil, skimming off any scum that forms. Add the turmeric, garlic, ginger and a little salt. Simmer, covered, for 40 minutes, giving the pot an occasional stir.

After the lentils have been cooking for about 30 minutes, heat the oil and butter for the tarka. Add the whole dried chillies and cumin seeds and, once they have browned, add the onion; sauté until well-browned. Add the tomatoes, garam masala and a little more salt and sauté until the masala releases oil, around 10 minutes. Pour some of the lentils into this pan, swirl and scrape the base to extract all the flavours, then pour everything back into the lentils.

Cook for another 10 minutes, mashing some of the lentils on the side of the pan to make a homogenous dhal. Add a little water if the lentils are too thick (remember it will thicken further as it cools). Taste, adjust the seasoning and serve scattered with the chopped coriander.

serves 4

for the dhal
100g Bengal gram (*chana dal*)
50g red lentils (*masur dal*)
½ tsp turmeric
3 fat garlic cloves, grated into a paste
10g fresh root ginger, peeled weight, grated into a paste
salt, to taste
handful of chopped fresh coriander leaves

for the tarka
3 tbsp vegetable oil
1 rounded tbsp butter
2–4 dried red chillies
1 rounded tsp cumin seeds
1 small onion, finely chopped
2 small tomatoes, chopped
½–¾ tsp garam masala, or to taste

punjabi yogurt and dumpling kadhi

This type of yogurt curry seems to exist in most northern, dairy-producing regions of India. Everyone has their own version, which might be sweeter, tangier, thinner, thicker or even contain coconut. This is the Punjabi version I grew up with and I do – objectively, of course! – think it is the best. It is full of flavour, the dumplings are earthy and give a toothsome, protein-filled bite to the smooth curry. Serve with rice.

Using your hands, mix together all the ingredients for the dumplings, adding 2½–3 tbsp water, or enough to make a thick, clinging paste. Set aside; the onions will soften as they stand. For the curry, stir the gram flour and yogurt until it is lump-free. Gradually add 700ml water to make a smooth paste.

Heat the 2 tbsp oil in a large non-stick saucepan. Add the whole spices and, once the light seeds have browned well, the onion, ginger, garlic, curry leaves and whole dried chillies or chilli powder. Sauté gently until the onions have softened. Add the yogurt mix and bring to a boil, stirring constantly to ensure it doesn't split. Add the powdered spices and tomato, stir well for another three or four minutes, then simmer for 30 minutes, stirring occasionally.

Meanwhile, pour enough oil into a small-medium saucepan to come 5–7.5cm up the sides, and heat until it is a moderate temperature for deep-frying: a drop of dumpling batter dropped in should sizzle immediately. Make small walnut-sized balls out of the dumpling mixture and add each to the oil. Do not overcrowd the pan (if your pan is small, do it in two batches). Keep the heat low so they fry evenly for seven or eight minutes and become a lovely golden brown, turning them in the oil. Drain on kitchen paper.

Once the curry is cooked, add the dumplings. The curry should have a consistency between single and double cream (add a splash of water if it's too thick, or cook some off if it seems watery). Season well, taste and add lemon juice; the kadhi should be tangy. Cook for another five minutes and serve, scattered with chopped fresh coriander and sliced green chillies, if you like.

serves 4

variations Add a handful of shredded spinach or any other green vegetable to the dumplings, as well as green chillies and fresh coriander leaves. Or omit the dumplings and add more vegetables - such as spinach, carrots, peas and cauliflower - to the curry instead.

for the dumplings
80g gram flour
½ tsp baking powder
½ onion, halved and finely sliced
¼ tsp salt
⅓ tsp carom seeds
⅓ tsp garam masala
⅓ tsp cumin seeds

for the curry
35g gram flour
200g plain yogurt (ideally a bit sour)
2 tbsp vegetable oil, plus more to
    deep-fry
2 cloves
½ tsp fenugreek seeds
¾ tsp mustard seeds
¾ tsp cumin seeds
½ onion, finely sliced
7g fresh root ginger, peeled weight,
    chopped
2 small garlic cloves, chopped
8 fresh curry leaves
1–2 dried red chillies, or a little chilli
    powder
⅓ tsp turmeric
1 tsp garam masala
1 tomato, cut into 8 pieces
salt, to taste
1–2 tbsp lemon juice, or to taste
    (depending on the tartness of the
    yogurt)
a little chopped fresh coriander
    and sliced green chilli, to serve
    (optional)

bengali-style mixed vegetables

Inspired by a Bengali staple called *shukto*, this is a mild dish with a mix of sweet, starchy vegetables as well as an essential bitter one, which was originally added to whet the appetite for future courses. I have used autumnal vegetables here, but this is not a heavy dish and is often eaten in the summer in Bengal. You can substitute any other vegetables, as long as you include some sweet and some bitter. I've used western vegetables here instead of the traditional Indian green bananas and bitter gourd, but the dish still works beautifully. Serve with rice.

3 tbsp white poppy seeds
1½ tbsp yellow mustard seeds
½ tsp brown mustard seeds
5 tbsp vegetable oil
1 tsp panch phoran
225g parsnips, peeled, cored and cut into 1.5cm half moons
225g sweet potato, peeled and cut into 1.5cm half moons
15g fresh root ginger, peeled weight, grated into a paste
3 long, thin aubergines (around 150g), or round aubergines, halved lengthways and cut into 2–3 pieces
15–20 green beans, topped, tailed and halved
salt, to taste
50g radicchio, endive or other bitter vegetable, diced
½–¾ tsp ground cumin
2 handfuls of cooked chickpeas
150ml full-fat milk
½ tsp sugar, or to taste

Using a spice grinder, grind the poppy and both types of mustard seeds to a fine powder. Set aside.

Heat the oil, add the panch phoran and, once it splutters, tip in the parsnips and sweet potatoes and sauté over a moderate flame for five to six minutes, or until softening. Add the ginger paste, aubergines, beans and salt and sauté for another three minutes. Add the bitter leaves, ground seeds, cumin and 200ml water. Bring to a boil, cover, reduce the heat and cook for three or four minutes, until all the ingredients are tender.

Uncover, add the chickpeas, then reduce most of liquid in the pan over high heat, stirring so nothing catches on the base. Add the milk and sugar, bring to a boil, taste, adjust the seasoning and serve.

serves 4

southern potato curry, two ways

This is a really delicious curry that you can tailor to your own tastes. If you like north Indian flavours, you can leave out the curry leaves and coconut milk and just add water. If you prefer the flavours of the south west coast, leave them in. The dish is wonderful either way. We would eat this with Indian fried breads (puris or Bhaturas, see page 150) for lunch, to give us plenty of time to digest the meal, but any flatbreads will do, or even some buttered toast. The sauce should have a light and creamy consistency, not too thin and not too thick.

Halve the potatoes and boil until just tender, (they will break up in the sauce if overcooked now). I prefer to boil them in their skins, to minimise the amount of water they absorb, then peel them before continuing.

Meanwhile, heat the oil in a large saucepan and add the mustard and cumin seeds, the lentils and cinnamon stick. Once the popping of the mustard seeds has died down, add the curry leaves (if using). Follow immediately with the onions and cook until soft and lightly golden.

Add the ginger, tomatoes, chilli, coriander, fennel, turmeric and salt and stir-fry over a high heat for three minutes. Add 200ml water, bring to a boil and simmer gently for 10 minutes. Add the cooked potatoes to the sauce to absorb the flavours for five minutes, or until the liquid in the pan has dried up.

Add the coconut milk (if using) and enough water to get a medium consistency sauce. Taste, adjust the seasoning and stir in the chopped coriander. Serve.

serves 4

500g potatoes
4 tbsp vegetable oil
$\frac{2}{3}$ tsp brown mustard seeds
$\frac{2}{3}$ tsp cumin seeds
1½ tsp Bengal gram (*chana dal*), washed and dried
5cm cinnamon stick
12 fresh curry leaves (optional, see recipe introduction)
2 small onions, finely chopped
10g fresh root ginger, peeled weight, finely chopped
2 large tomatoes, chopped
¼–½ tsp chilli powder
2 rounded tsp ground coriander
½ tsp fennel seeds, ground
$\frac{1}{3}$ tsp turmeric
salt, to taste
150ml coconut milk (optional, see recipe introduction)
large handful of chopped fresh coriander, to serve

paneer and pepper karahi

Paneer is a homemade white cheese, similar to ricotta and mozzarella in taste but firm enough to cut into cubes. It's really easy, can be prepared in advance and very satisfying to create (see page 25). You can buy ready-made blocks of paneer in many well-stocked supermarkets and Indian stores, but it won't be as good as homemade. This dish is full of flavours and textures and makes a fantastic vegetarian main course. Serve with Naan (see page 155) or Paratha (see page 157).

Heat the oil in a large non-stick saucepan or karahi. Add the cumin seeds and cook until they have darkened and released their aromas. Add the ginger and garlic pastes and gently sauté for a minute, or until the garlic smells cooked. Add the onion and green chillies and sauté for another minute.

Add the tomatoes and all the spices and season. Cook over a high heat, stirring often, for 10-15 minutes, until the mixture is cooked and releases some oil back into the pan. Taste; the flavours should be harmonious.

Stir in the paneer, peppers and a good splash of water from the kettle. Cook for three or four minutes, or until the peppers are crisp but tender and the sauce is thick and clinging to the vegetables. Add the cream, taste and adjust the seasoning, and serve.

serves 4–6

6 tbsp vegetable oil
1½ tsp cumin seeds
12g fresh root ginger, peeled weight, grated into a paste
2 garlic cloves, grated into a paste
1 smallish onion, roughly diced
3–4 green chillies, whole but pierced
3 small tomatoes, blended until smooth or chopped
⅓ tsp turmeric
¼–½ tsp chilli powder
3 tsp ground coriander
¾ tsp ground cumin
1 tsp garam masala
salt, to taste
2 x recipe Fresh Paneer (see page 25), or 300g shop-bought paneer, cut into 2.5cm dice
½ each small green and red pepper, cut into 2.5cm dice
2–3 tbsp single cream

aubergine in a creamy peanut sauce

This is such a delicious dish that it is renowned across India. It is an orchestra of flavours; sweet, tangy, nutty, spicy and salty, one of those meals that even meat-eaters crave. It is rich so, though it takes less than 20 minutes to make, it is one to serve as a treat to friends. As aubergines collapse when cooked, Indians use small whole vegetables and make a deep cross from the base to just under the stalk – without cutting the aubergine into pieces – so you can see the whole vegetable and the insides get flavoured too. Serve with Indian breads or a pilaf.

1 tbsp coriander seeds
1½ tbsp sesame seeds
4 tbsp unsweetened desiccated coconut
7 tbsp lightly roasted or raw peanuts
5 tbsp vegetable oil
1 largish onion, sliced
10g fresh root ginger, peeled weight, roughly chopped
¾ tsp mustard seeds
¾ tsp cumin seeds
½ tsp nigella seeds
pinch of fenugreek seeds
450g Japanese aubergines (around 8), or small round aubergines, quartered but left attached at the stalk end (see recipe introduction)
salt, to taste
½ tsp turmeric
⅓–⅔ tsp chilli powder
1 tbsp sugar or jaggery, or to taste
1¼–1¾ tsp tamarind paste
a little chopped fresh coriander, to serve

In a small pan, gently dry roast the coriander seeds until they turn a light brown. Pour straight into a spice grinder or mortar. Add the sesame seeds and coconut to the pan and dry roast these until the coconut is golden. Add to the coriander seeds. Toast the peanuts (if raw) in the same way. Add the peanuts to the seeds and coconut and whizz or pestle to a fine powder.

Heat half the oil in a large saucepan. Add the onion and, once it is soft and colouring on the edges, the ginger. Once the onions are a lovely golden brown, spoon the whole lot into a blender, leaving behind the oil, and add the ground nut powder and 150ml water. Blend until smooth.

Pour the remaining oil into the pan and add the remaining whole spices. Once the fenugreek seeds have browned, add the aubergines, give them a good stir in the oil and pour in the onion paste with 350ml water, the salt, turmeric, chilli powder and sugar. Bring to a boil, cover and cook gently for 10–15 minutes, or until the aubergine is soft. The sauce should be like double cream and thickens as it sits so, if necessary, add a splash of water from the kettle.

Add the tamarind and adjust the seasoning and sugar to taste, and serve sprinkled with chopped coriander.

serves 4

traditionally…the aubergine would be lightly shallow-fried before being added to the sauce. I have left out this step to cut down on the oil, but the crispy texture is nice. I'll leave it up to you.

tangy chickpea curry

Whenever I translate the Indian name of this dish literally into English it comes out as 'bean curry', which is misleadingly and depressingly reminiscent of the sandal-wearing hippies of the 1960s and 1970s and detracts from its Indian roots and utter deliciousness. A lovely, flavourful dish, it's great with Bhatura (see page 158) for a fabulous weekend lunch. But I often eat it with buttered wholemeal bread for a divine, simple meal.

Blend together the ginger, garlic and tomatoes with a little water until smooth (I use a stick blender). Set aside.

Heat the oil in a large saucepan. Add the cloves, cardamom pods, cinnamon and half the cumin seeds and cook until they release their aroma and start to crackle. Add the green chillies and onion and cook until the onion is well browned. Add the tomato paste with the turmeric, ground coriander, chilli powder and salt and cook over a moderate to high heat until the oil comes out at the sides (around 15 minutes), stirring often.

Meanwhile, use the remaining cumin seeds to make roasted cumin powder (see below). Add it to the pot.

Add the chickpeas and 500ml water. Bring to a boil then simmer over a medium heat for seven or eight minutes. Stir in the garam masala and tamarind paste. Mash a few of the chickpeas on the side of the pan to thicken the sauce a little. Taste for seasoning and tartness, adjusting if necessary, then sprinkle with the chopped coriander and serve.

serves 4–5

to make roasted cumin powder roast cumin seeds in a small dry pan for about 40 seconds, stirring constantly, until they have darkened quite a bit. Grind to a fine powder.

12g fresh root ginger, peeled weight
4 fat garlic cloves
2 largish tomatoes, quartered
5–6 tbsp vegetable oil
4 cloves
4 green cardamom pods
1 black cardamom pod
2 large shards of cinnamon
2 tsp cumin seeds
2–3 green chillies, whole but pierced
1 onion, finely chopped
½ tsp turmeric
1 tbsp ground coriander
¼–½ tsp chilli powder
salt, to taste
2 x 400g cans of chickpeas, drained
   and rinsed
1¼ tsp garam masala
½–⅔ tsp tamarind paste, or dried
   pomegranate powder, or to taste
handful of finely chopped fresh
   coriander

light tofu and pea curry

This is a dish I eat regularly as it tastes good and is healthy. It is based on the classic *mattar paneer* (paneer with peas) but, as paneer can be heavy, I've substituted tofu for years. Though it has a completely different taste, it is still a vegetarian protein and absorbs other flavours in the same way, so works well here. You can, of course, use paneer instead if you prefer. I eat this with brown rice.

12g fresh root ginger, peeled weight
3 garlic cloves
2 tomatoes, quartered
2 tbsp vegetable oil
¾ tsp cumin seeds
8 black peppercorns
3 cloves
5cm cinnamon stick
1 large bay leaf
1 onion, finely chopped
½ tsp turmeric
⅛–¼ tsp chilli powder, or to taste
2 level tsp ground coriander
salt, to taste
200g peas
200g firm tofu, cut into cubes
100ml whole milk
small handful of chopped fresh
   coriander leaves

Make a smooth paste of the ginger, garlic and tomatoes, using a little water to help (I use a stick blender).

Heat the vegetable oil in a non-stick saucepan. Add the whole spices and bay leaf and, once the cumin seeds have darkened, tip in the onion and cook until golden brown. Add the tomato paste, turmeric, chilli, coriander and salt. Bring to a boil and cook over a moderate flame until the paste releases oil droplets on the base of the pan, around 10 minutes, then gently sauté the paste for a further five or six minutes; it will deepen in colour and flavour.

Add the peas and tofu and stir for two or three minutes. Add the milk with 350ml water and bring to a boil. Simmer for five or six minutes, or until the curry has a light, creamy consistency. Taste, adjust the seasoning and serve, scattered with chopped coriander.

serves 3–4 moderately

fluffy spinach koftas in a creamy tomato curry

A kofta was traditionally a meatball, but the vegetarian masses of India (perhaps the most inventive cooks I've ever come across) soon started to make their own versions. These would have been made with paneer but I didn't want to add the extra work, so I tried it with ricotta instead. The resulting koftas are light, fluffy and absolutely delicious with this full-bodied, lightly spiced sauce. Serve with pilaf (see pages 160-163) or Naan (see page 155).

Blend together the tomatoes, garlic and ginger to a fine paste, using a little water to help; I use a stick blender. Heat the 5 tbsp of oil in a large non-stick saucepan. Add the onion and cook until lightly browned. Add the tomato paste, cashew nuts, spices and salt. Cook over a moderate heat for around 15 minutes, stirring occasionally, until the paste releases oil. Blend until smooth with a stick blender, adding a little water, if necessary, to help. Pour back into the pan, add 500ml water, bring to a boil and simmer for eight to 10 minutes, until the curry is the consistency of single cream.

While the curry is cooking, make the dumplings. Wilt the spinach in a pan with a little water and a good pinch of salt. Once cool enough to handle, squeeze out the excess water and blend to a coarse puree with a stick blender. Add the cornflour and ricotta and stir well.

Heat the oil for deep-frying in a wide sauté pan or a karahi. There should be enough to come 5cm up the sides of the sauté pan, or 10cm up the sides of a small karahi. Test the oil temperature by dropping in a small amount of the spinach mixture; it should sizzle immediately but not colour straight away. Drop heaped teaspoonfuls of the mixture straight into the oil. You may need to do this in batches, so as not to crowd the pan. You should be able to make about 20. Carefully cook them, turning to ensure even cooking; they take about seven or eight minutes and will (unfortunately) turn brown, losing their vivid green colour. Remove and blot off excess oil on kitchen paper.

Once the dumplings are all cooked, place them in the curry and cook for five minutes. Stir in the cream or butter (if using) and serve.

serves 4-5

for the curry
2 large tomatoes, quartered and deseeded
3 garlic cloves
10g fresh root ginger, peeled weight
5 tbsp vegetable oil, plus more to deep-fry
1 onion, sliced
40g cashew nuts
½ tsp turmeric
¼–½ tsp chilli powder for heat, or ½ tsp paprika for colour
1¼ tsp ground coriander
1 tsp ground cumin
1 tsp garam masala
salt, to taste
2–3 tbsp double cream, or a knob of butter (optional)

for the koftas
200g spinach, I use whole leaf (not baby leaf) for more flavour, well washed
2 tbsp cornflour
200g ricotta cheese

fish and
seafood

green sindhi fish curry

A lovely dish that is everyday fare for the Sindhi community. It is quick and easy and the flavour is herby, deep and rich, but doesn't overpower the fish. This same sauce is also used to cook leftover rotis and pieces of bread, so I would serve this with Indian flatbreads or even lightly buttered bread.

4 tbsp vegetable oil
1 smallish onion, sliced
20g fresh coriander leaves and stalks
4 garlic cloves
10g fresh root ginger, peeled weight
1 tomato, chopped
salt, to taste
1 rounded tsp ground coriander
2–4 green chillies, whole but pierced
3 fillets of firm white fish, left whole
    or cut into large cubes

Heat the oil in a non-stick saucepan. Add the onion and cook until well browned. Remove from the heat.

Blend together the coriander leaves and stalks, garlic, ginger and cooked onion with a little water until smooth. Pour back into the saucepan along with the tomato, salt, ground coriander and chillies. Add 150ml water, bring to a boil, cover and cook for 20 minutes, stirring occasionally.

Uncover, reduce any remaining water by boiling hard, then sauté until the oil leaves the masala. Add 250ml water and the fish, bring to a boil, then reduce the heat and simmer gently for three or four minutes, or until the fish is cooked through. Taste, adjust the seasoning and serve.

serves 3–4

bengali mustard fish

A classic, this is absolutely terrific and so different from other fish curries. It has very few ingredients, so they all play an important part. The fish should be in steaks so that they do not break up when you fry them, and the bones will ensure extra flavour. You can also use sea bass, bream or tilapia. The dish will not taste as good without the green chillies, so try it with them: you might find it spicy, but I bet you can't stop eating! Mustard seeds can be bitter if overworked, so grind them only briefly in a spice grinder. Measure this powder, not the seeds, before adding it to the curry. Serve with plain boiled rice.

450g halibut steaks, left whole
   or quartered
¾ tsp turmeric
salt, to taste
1½ small tomatoes (around 150g)
3 fat garlic cloves
4–5 green chillies (preferably Indian
   finger)
1½ tbsp powdered brown mustard
   seeds (see recipe introduction)
4 tbsp mustard or vegetable oil
1¼ tsp nigella seeds
handful of fresh coriander leaves

Marinate the fish in ¼ tsp of the turmeric and a good pinch of salt, tossing with your hands to coat.

Meanwhile, blend the tomatoes, garlic and two or three of the green chillies (deseeded if you are worried about their heat), a little more salt, the powdered mustard seeds, remaining turmeric and 150ml water to a smooth paste.

If using mustard oil, heat 3 tbsp in a non-stick pan until smoking, then remove from the heat and wait for 30 seconds before proceeding with the recipe. If using vegetable oil, simply heat 3 tbsp of the oil. Add the nigella seeds and, once they have sizzled for 10 seconds, put in the tomato-chilli-mustard paste.

Cook over a moderate flame until all the excess moisture has evaporated and the paste releases oil, stirring occasionally. Then reduce the heat and continue cooking for four minutes or so until it darkens a little. Add 400ml water and the remaining chillies; bring to a boil and simmer for seven or eight minutes. It should not be too watery, so cook until it has a medium consistency. Check the seasoning and keep it on a low heat.

Heat the remaining oil in a frying pan until smoking. Add the fish and fry well on all sides for about six minutes, until golden brown. Now put the fish in the mustard sauce, bring back to a boil and cook for two minutes. Gently shake in the coriander leaves and serve.

serves 3–4

crab curry

My brother-in-law has been telling me about his mother's crab curry for years so, when I started to work on this recipe, I invited him over and we cooked together as we reminisced about our mothers' food. This lovely curry is the product of that fun, disjointed Saturday afternoon. If the whole peppercorns and cloves bother you, strain the sauce to remove them before pouring it over the crab. This curry improves after sitting for a few hours, as the sauce seeps into the crab. I buy my crab fresh from my fishmonger who kindly cleans and cuts it up for me. I add about 4–5 tbsp of the brown meat for extra flavour, but you can add more or less, as you prefer.

2 x 750g whole raw crabs, cleaned
    and cut into pieces
7 tbsp vegetable oil
20 fenugreek seeds
8 cloves
20 black peppercorns
15 fresh curry leaves
2–4 green chillies, whole but pierced
2 largish onions, chopped
10 large garlic cloves
4 small tomatoes, quartered
15g fresh root ginger, peeled weight
salt, to taste
¼–½ tsp chilli powder
2 tsp ground coriander
2 level tsp ground cumin
½ tsp turmeric
1–1½ tsp tamarind paste, or to taste
200ml coconut milk (optional)

Ask your fishmonger to clean the crabs, smash the claws slightly so you can get at the meat later, and to halve or quarter the bodies. He will also give you the brown meat separately, if you ask nicely.

Heat the oil in a large non-stick saucepan or karahi. Add the fenugreek, cloves and peppercorns and, once the fenugreek has browned, the curry leaves.

Tip in the green chillies and onions and cook until golden. Meanwhile, blend together the garlic, tomatoes, ginger and a good splash of water until smooth. Add to the pot with the salt, chilli, coriander, cumin and turmeric. Bring to a boil and simmer until the masala releases oil into the pan, then gently stir-fry for a further five to seven minutes to intensify the flavours.

Add 800ml water and bring to a boil. Stir in the tamarind paste. Add the crab pieces and brown meat, bring back to a boil, cover and simmer over a moderate heat for about 15 minutes, until the crab is cooked. There should only be a little liquid left. Stir in the coconut milk (if using) and add a little boiled water if you think the dish needs more sauce. Taste and adjust the seasoning, adding more tamarind to taste, then serve.

serves 4

prawn patia

This is a great fruity, sweet, sour and spicy curry, served on special occasions in Parsi homes with a simple yellow lentil curry and white rice. But it needn't be saved for best, as it's not hard to make. Kashmiri chillies are known for their deep red colour and mild heat. I found mine in a well-stocked local supermarket – which was lucky – but you can also buy them in Indian stores or on the internet, and they last really well in the larder. If you can't find any, use 1–2 normal dried red chillies. Sambhar powder is a spice blend usually used in this dish to add an extra punch of flavour, though I have to admit that I don't generally have any, so it's not essential.

4–7 dried Kashmiri chillies, stalks and seeds removed
6 tbsp vegetable oil
2 onions, finely sliced
3 largish tomatoes, quartered
5 large garlic cloves
1 rounded tsp ground coriander
1½ tsp ground cumin
⅓ tsp turmeric
½ good tsp garam masala
½ tsp sambhar powder (optional)
salt, to taste
2–2½ tsp grated jaggery, or sugar, to taste
1¼–1¾ tsp tamarind paste, or to taste
400g raw prawns, shelled, deveined and rinsed
handful of chopped fresh coriander leaves

Soak the dried chillies in hot water for 30 minutes.

Heat the oil in a deep saute pan. Add the onions and cook for 10–12 minutes, until really quite brown.

Meanwhile, blend together the tomatoes, garlic and soaked chillies until you have a fine paste. Add to the pan with 350ml water, the spices and salt. Bring to a boil and cook, stirring occasionally, for 20 minutes. It will get really thick and darken considerably; stir more often as it thickens.

Stir in the jaggery or sugar, most of the tamarind and a good splash of water. Bring to a boil; the sauce should still be quite thick. Add the prawns and cook for two or three minutes until done. Taste and adjust the seasoning, adding more sweet jaggery or sour tamarind to taste. Sprinkle over the chopped coriander and serve.

serves 4

creamy tomato fish curry

This is a lovely, mild dish whose star ingredients are sweet-sour tomatoes and, of course, the fish. It is easy to cook for a delicious midweek meal, but also elegant enough to impress your friends. You can choose any fish you like; I like to use fish steaks in most of my curries, but monkfish also works well (though if you use monkfish, don't fry it before adding to the curry; just tip it straight in). This is lovely with a pilaf or Indian flatbreads (see Breads and Rice, page 154).

Rub half the turmeric and a good pinch of salt into the fish and leave to marinate as you cook the sauce.

Heat 5 tbsp of the oil in a non-stick saucepan. Add the whole spices and bay leaves and, once they have sizzled for 10 seconds, the onion. Cook until golden brown.

Meanwhile, blend the tomatoes, ginger and garlic until smooth, adding a splash of water to help, if needed. Add this paste to the pan with all the spices (except the garam masala) and salt, to taste. Cook over a medium-high flame, stirring often, for 10–12 minutes, until the spice mix (masala) releases oil droplets. Reduce the heat and brown the paste for a further six minutes to intensify the flavours. Add 500ml water and bring to a boil, reduce the heat and simmer for six or seven minutes. Taste and adjust the seasoning.

Meanwhile fry the fish. Heat the remaining oil in a frying pan until very hot. Add the marinated pieces of fish and cook, undisturbed, for two minutes. Turn and cook for another two minutes or so, until golden brown. Add the fried fish, garam masala and cream to the curry. Simmer for another three minutes so the fish finishes cooking and starts to absorb the sauce. Taste, adjust the seasoning and serve scattered with chopped coriander.

serves 4

1 tsp turmeric
salt, to taste
500–550g firm white fish steaks, such as halibut, halved
7 tbsp vegetable oil
6 cloves
6 green cardamom pods
12 black peppercorns
2 bay leaves
1 small onion, finely chopped
4 tomatoes, quartered and deseeded
10g fresh root ginger, peeled weight
6 fat garlic cloves
¼–½ tsp chilli powder
1 tbsp ground coriander
freshly ground black pepper, to taste
¾ tsp garam masala
2 tbsp single cream
handful of fresh coriander leaves, chopped

mild prawn curry with cashew nuts

A lovely, delicate curry inspired by the Christian dishes and ingredients of Kerala. It is easy, quick and great for family (without the chilli) or friends. The cashew nuts are lightly roasted, then added to the prawns, but you can leave them out. The Keralans would use a thin extract of coconut milk to cook the prawns, then add thicker coconut milk at the end. Canned coconut milk should have its cream accumulated at the top, so spoon this off and stir it in at the end; it adds a lovely aroma and richness.

Blend the ginger and garlic to a fine paste, adding a little water to help. Heat 1 tsp of the oil in a non-stick saucepan; add the cashew nuts and stir-fry until golden. Remove with a slotted spoon, toss in a little salt and set aside.

Add the rest of the oil to the pan. Once hot, add the fenugreek and mustard seeds; they will start popping. Once the noise dies down a little, add the onion and cook gently until soft. Add the ginger and garlic paste and cook until any excess moisture dries up, then reduce the heat and stir over a low flame for two minutes or so, until the garlic smells cooked.

Add the spices and chillies, salt and a splash of water. Once the water has dried up, add 250ml of the thinner part of the coconut milk (see recipe introduction), 100ml water and the vinegar.

Bring to a boil, then simmer for 10 minutes. Taste, adjust the seasoning and tartness (if the garlic was still raw, you will be able to taste it here. If it is, cook for another five minutes, then check again). The sauce should have the consistency of single cream.

Add the prawns and cook until done; in around three minutes they will have curled up and become opaque. Stir in the remaining, thicker coconut milk and the cashews. Serve with rice.

serves 4, can be halved

30g fresh root ginger, peeled weight, roughly chopped
6 fat garlic cloves, halved
5 tbsp vegetable oil
60g raw cashew nuts
salt, to taste
scant ½ tsp fenugreek seeds
scant 1 tsp mustard seeds
1 onion, sliced
1 rounded tbsp ground coriander
¾ tsp turmeric
generous ¾–1 tsp ground black pepper
1 tsp ground cumin
4–6 red or green chillies, or to taste, left whole or slit for more heat
400ml creamy coconut milk
2 tbsp white wine vinegar, or to taste
350g large raw prawns, shelled, deveined and rinsed

authentic goan fish curry

This is delicious. Many coconut curries are mild – there are several in this book – so here I give a spicy example. Use a firm white fish such as halibut, tilapia or monkfish. You can use boneless pieces, but bear in mind they must stand up to cooking in a curry without breaking up. Serve with rice.

Using a spice grinder, grind the cumin seeds, dried chillies and coriander seeds to a fine powder.

Heat the oil in a large non-stick saucepan. Add the onion and cook over a medium flame until golden.

Meanwhile, blend together the ginger, garlic and tomatoes until smooth, adding a little water to help. Add to the onions and cook over a medium flame for eight to 10 minutes, until the paste releases oil droplets on the base of the pan. Add the ground whole spices, turmeric and salt along with a small splash of water and cook for two minutes. Add the coconut milk and 300ml water, bring to a boil and simmer for a few minutes.

Add the tamarind paste, green chillies and fish, bring back to a boil and simmer gently until the fish is just done; it will take three to six minutes, depending on the cut and type of fish. Add the coconut cream and shake the pan to incorporate. Taste, adjust the salt and tamarind until the balance is perfect for you, then serve.

serves 4

2 scant tsp cumin seeds
4–7 Kashmiri (mild) dried red chillies, seeds shaken out
4 tsp coriander seeds
3 tbsp vegetable oil
1 small onion, finely chopped
30g fresh root ginger, peeled weight, cut into large chunks
6 fat garlic cloves
1 small tomato, quartered
¾ tsp turmeric
salt, to taste
100ml coconut milk
1 tsp tamarind paste, or to taste
2–4 green chillies (preferably Indian finger), whole but pierced
600g firm white fish steaks or fillets (see recipe introduction)
4 good tbsp coconut cream (I find mine in cartons)

north indian-spiced prawn curry

This is one of my favourite ways to eat prawns. The tomato- and garlic-based sauce is lightly spiced and there is a lot of flavour, but not so much that it dominates the sweet prawns. This is lovely with rice or Indian breads, or even a piece of buttered, crusty bread to dip into the sauce. Mustard oil adds a further layer of flavour; if you use it, bring it to smoking point then take off the heat for 30 seconds to cool before continuing.

Blend the tomatoes, garlic and 5g of the ginger to a fine puree. Finely slice the remaining ginger into julienne.

Heat the oil in a large, non-stick saucepan, add the panch phoran and let it sizzle for 10–15 seconds, or until the lighter seeds have become a warm brown colour. Add the onion, chillies and ginger julienne and cook until the onions are lightly golden.

Add the tomato paste, remaining spices and salt. Cook over a moderate heat for around 15 minutes until the spice paste releases oil, stirring often as it thickens. Taste, it should be well-balanced and harmonious. Add the prawns and enough water to cover them by half. Bring to a boil, then simmer gently for three or four minutes, until the prawns are done. The sauce should be light but not watery. Stir in the cream, taste and adjust the seasoning, adding lemon juice if you like, and serve with the chopped coriander.

serves 4–5

2 tomatoes
5 fat garlic cloves
12g ginger, peeled weight
5 tbsp mustard or vegetable oil
1 rounded tsp panch phoran
1 small onion, finely chopped
1–3 green chillies (preferably Indian finger), whole but pierced
1½ tsp ground coriander
⅓ tsp turmeric
¼ tsp chilli powder
1 tsp garam masala
¾ tsp ground cumin
salt, to taste
400g large raw prawns, shelled, deveined and rinsed
1 tbsp double cream
1–2 tsp lemon juice, or to taste (depends on the tartness of your tomatoes)
handful of chopped fresh coriander leaves, to serve

creamy keralan seafood curry

This lovely, harmonious coconut sauce goes perfectly with seafood. I use an assortment here as I like the different textures and flavours that a good variety of seafood offers. Or you can also use the same amount of firm white-fleshed fish instead. This is a wonderful dish; serve it with rice.

Heat the oil in a large sauté pan. Add the mustard seeds and peppercorns and, once they have popped, the curry leaves, onion and chillies. Cook until the onions are just soft and turning golden. Add the ginger and garlic and sauté for a couple of minutes on a gentle heat.

Add the tomatoes, spices and salt and cook for seven or eight minutes until the paste releases oil. Add the coconut milk and 250ml water. Bring to a boil and simmer for five minutes.

The sauce should have a consistency just thicker than single cream (if necessary reduce it a little more to thicken, or add a splash of water to loosen). Add the tamarind and follow with the seafood. Cook gently until done, around three minutes (if using crab claws, they may need to be added first to cook a little longer), then stir in the reserved coconut cream. Taste and adjust the seasoning, chilli heat and tamarind, to taste, then serve.

serves 4

5 tbsp coconut or vegetable oil
1 rounded tsp mustard seeds
10 black peppercorns
15 fresh curry leaves
1 onion, finely chopped
2–4 green chillies, whole but pierced
20g fresh root ginger, peeled weight, grated into a paste
5 fat garlic cloves, grated into a paste
2 tomatoes, blended to a paste or chopped
½ tsp chilli powder, or to taste
¾ tsp turmeric
1 good tbsp ground coriander
1 tsp ground cumin
salt, to taste
400ml creamy coconut milk (reserve 2 tbsp of the cream that accumulates on top)
¾–1 tsp tamarind paste, or to taste
500g assorted raw seafood (prawns, mussels, squid rings, crab claws), or white fish

fish caldine

This is a mild and creamy fish curry from Goa in spite of the long list of spices. If you do like the heat, add more than a couple of the dried chillies; I break them open and shake out the seeds before using. Or you can add a couple of red chillies to the oil before the onion to get some heat, then taste the sauce at any time and, if you find it has the right amount of heat, you can fish them out. Serve with rice.

Heat the oil in a non-stick saucepan. Add the onion and fry until golden. At the same time, using a spice grinder, make a fine powder of the chillies, all the whole spices and the poppy seeds or almonds. You can do this in a mortar and pestle, but remember it must be a fine powder.

Add the garlic and ginger to the onions and gently cook for a couple of minutes, until the raw smell of the garlic has disappeared. Add the spice powder, turmeric and salt and cook, stirring, for 40–50 seconds.

Add the coconut milk, 350ml water and the tamarind paste. Bring to a gentle boil and simmer for five minutes. Taste and adjust the seasoning. Add the fish and cook until done, anything from four to eight minutes depending on whether they are fillets or steaks. The sauce should be light and creamy; add a little boiling water if it is too thick. Serve scattered with chopped coriander.

serves 4

3 tbsp vegetable oil
1 smallish onion, sliced
1–3 dried red chillies, seeds shaken out (optional, see recipe introduction)
1 tsp cumin seeds
2 tsp coriander seeds
16 black peppercorns
2 cloves
2cm cinnamon stick
2 heaped tbsp white poppy seeds or ground almonds
6 fat garlic cloves, grated into a paste
10g ginger, peeled weight, grated into a paste
½ tsp turmeric
salt, to taste
320ml coconut milk, or more for a creamier curry
1 tsp tamarind paste, or to taste
450g fish steaks, or firm white fillets
handful of chopped fresh coriander leaves

prawn, mango and coconut curry

An unusual curry that came to life after a chat with my publisher who wanted to include mangoes in the book, particularly in a savoury curry. It was not something I had tried, but I gave it some thought and this slightly sweet, slightly hot curry is the delicious result of that conversation. It works really well, cooks in less than 10 minutes and is lovely with rice in late spring when mangoes come into season.

Blend the powdered mustard seeds with 100ml water. This helps the powder to become more of a paste and incorporates more easily with the sauce.

Heat the oil in a large non-stick saucepan and add the whole mustard seeds. Once they have popped, add the curry leaves, black peppercorns and whole chillies. Follow five seconds later with the coconut milk, mustard seed paste, salt, sugar, rice powder and 300ml water. Bring to a boil and simmer for five minutes. Add the prawns and simmer for two minutes more. Add the mango and cook for another minute. Taste, adjust the seasoning and sugar to taste and serve sprinkled with chopped coriander.

... or a vegetarian version Instead of prawns, you can add two handfuls of raw cashew nuts. I know it sounds odd, but on the west coast of India they cook a similar dish with pineapples or mangoes and nuts. It is eaten instead of lentils; the cashews provide the protein and it makes a delicious side dish.

serves 4

1 tsp powdered brown mustard
  seeds (see page 62)
3 tbsp vegetable oil
1 tsp brown mustard seeds
15 fresh curry leaves
10 black peppercorns
5–7 dried red chillies
350–375ml coconut milk
salt, to taste
1½–2 tsp sugar, or to taste
1 rounded tsp rice powder
350g medium or large raw prawns,
  peeled, deveined and rinsed
2 ripe (but not mushy) mangoes,
  peeled and cut into squares
handful of chopped fresh coriander

bengali yogurt fish

One of Bengal's most popular dishes, and deservedly so. It is absolutely delicious: creamy, but not heavy, and delicately spiced. I have added tomatoes as I think it tastes better. Fresh water fish would be perfect in this dish, but I have cooked it many ways and most firm-fleshed white fish work well. It goes brilliantly with both rice and Indian breads.

Heat the oil in a saucepan. Add the onion and cook until soft and lightly golden. Add the ginger and garlic pastes and cook over a gentle flame for around two minutes, stirring often; the garlic should smell cooked. Stir in the spices, salt and green chillies. Pour in the pureed tomatoes and 150ml water and cook over a moderate flame until the liquid has evaporated, then continue stirring until the tomato takes on the rich colour of tomato puree. Stir in the yogurt until really well blended.

Pour in 200ml water, bring to a gentle boil, stirring constantly, then simmer for five to eight minutes, or until the sauce has the consistency of single cream. Taste; you may want more salt or chilli powder.

Add your fish and shake the pan to coat the fillets with the sauce. Cover and cook gently for three to five minutes, or until the fish is cooked through. Serve sprinkled with a little fresh coriander.

Serves 4, can be halved

5 tbsp vegetable oil
1 small onion, finely chopped
10g fresh root ginger, peeled weight, grated into a paste
2 fat garlic cloves, grated into a paste
¼–½ tsp chilli powder, or to taste
2 tsp ground coriander
salt, to taste
1–3 green chillies, stalks removed, left whole
2 small tomatoes, blended to a puree
2 heaped tbsp good Greek yogurt
500-600g firm white fish fillets, cut into fairly large pieces
a few fresh coriander leaves, chopped, to serve

mussels with saffron

This curry is a reflection of my childhood, as we spent many holidays in France and I have fond memories of eating light saffron-flavoured seafood dishes under the sun. I wanted to evoke those meals, but to give them a new life and zest with Indian flavours, particularly ginger and chillies. There is plenty of sauce to mop up with rice or a hunk of bread. Make sure the mussels are as fresh as can be and buy extra; even if you cook them the day you buy them, there are often a few that are unuseable. Any raw mussels that are open and do not close when firmly tapped on the counter should be thrown away, as should any that remain closed once cooked.

Heat the oil in a saucepan large enough to hold all the mussels. Add the peppercorns and follow with the onions, cooking them until lightly golden. Add the green chillies, ginger and garlic pastes and gently sauté until the garlic smells cooked; it should take about two minutes.

Add the tomatoes, spices and salt and cook, stirring often and lightly mashing the tomatoes with a spoon, for 10–12 minutes, or until you have a thick masala that has released oil back into the pan. Taste it; there should be no harsh flavours.

Add 500ml water and bring to a boil. Simmer for five minutes. Add the mussels, cover, shake, then simmer for three minutes or until the mussels have opened. Add the cream, taste and adjust the seasoning, saffron and ground fennel seed to taste. The sauce should be lightly creamy. If it is too watery, put your mussels in a warmed serving bowl while you boil the sauce to reduce it, then pour this back over the mussels. Stir in the chopped coriander and serve.

serves 4

4 tbsp vegetable oil
25 black peppercorns
2½ small onions, chopped
4–6 green chillies, whole but pierced
35g ginger, peeled weight, grated into a paste
5 garlic cloves, grated into a paste
2½ tomatoes, chopped
1 tsp fennel seeds, ground, or to taste
½ tsp turmeric
2 tsp ground coriander
good pinch of saffron (around 20-25 strands), slightly crumbled, or to taste
salt, to taste
1kg mussels, scrubbed and debearded
150ml double cream
a little chopped fresh coriander, to serve

karahi prawns

A karahi is a concave pan similar to a wok and, like wok cooking, a 'karahi' dish conjures up images of ingredients being tossed into the pan in quick succession and cooked over high heat. The resulting dish should be slightly caramelised in places but also retain lots of fresh flavours with a warm, rich sauce. Dried fenugreek leaves have a wonderful flavour and it is worth buying a packet as they keep really well for a year and can be used to enhance most north Indian dishes. Carom seeds are also known as *ajwain* and have a wonderful thyme-like taste that adds a special note. Serve with Indian breads.

5 tbsp ghee or vegetable oil
1 small onion, finely chopped
20g fresh root ginger, peeled weight, grated into a paste
7 fat garlic cloves, grated into a paste
2–4 fresh green chillies, whole but pierced
6 small tomatoes, chopped
1½ tsp ground coriander
1½ tsp ground cumin
¾ tsp carom seeds
2 tsp dried fenugreek leaves, crumbled
¼–½ tsp chilli powder, or to taste
400g large or medium raw prawns, peeled, deveined and rinsed
1½ tsp garam masala
1–2 tbsp single cream
salt and freshly ground pepper, to taste
handful of fresh coriander leaves
1 tsp lemon juice, or to taste

Heat 4 tbsp of the ghee or oil in a karahi or sauté pan. Add the onion and cook over a high heat until browned. Add the ginger and garlic pastes and chillies. Sauté gently for a minute or two, until the garlic smells cooked. Add the tomatoes, ground coriander and cumin, carom seeds, crumbled fenugreek leaves and chilli powder. Cook, stirring occasionally, for about 15 minutes, or until the oil comes out of the paste, then stir for three or four minutes more, or until the tomatoes have darkened a little. Set this masala aside.

Heat the remaining ghee or oil in the pan, add the prawns and sauté for a minute. Add the masala paste, garam masala, cream and 50ml water; cook for another two minutes. The sauce should be fairly thick and clinging to the prawns. Taste and adjust the seasoning. Stir in the coriander leaves and add lemon, to taste.

serves 4

poultry

punjabi chicken curry

I grew up eating this. It has a thin liquor rather than a thick sauce but is full of flavour. This recipe appears in *Anjum's New Indian* but I wanted to give it here too, as this is the curry I am most asked about and my book on curries wouldn't be complete without it. Please do use chicken on the bone as it really makes a difference, giving that lovely rounded flavour. If you have a friendly butcher, ask him to joint and skin the chicken for you. I use small chickens as I find them more succulent. Eat with Chapati (see page 156), or a pilaf.

15g fresh root ginger, peeled weight, cut into large pieces
10 fat garlic cloves
5 tbsp vegetable oil
5cm cinnamon stick
3 large black cardamom pods
4 green cardamom pods
4 cloves
2 bay leaves
1 onion, chopped
2–4 green chillies, whole but pierced
3 tomatoes (not too ripe), cut into thin wedges
salt, to taste
2 tbsp ground coriander
2 tsp ground cumin
½ tsp turmeric
¼–½ tsp chilli powder
1½ tsp garam masala
750g skinless chicken joints
large handful of chopped fresh coriander

Using a little water, make a fine paste of the ginger and garlic. Set aside.

Heat the oil in a large non-stick frying pan. Add the whole spices and bay leaves and, once they have sizzled for 10 seconds, add the onion and cook until golden brown. Add the chillies and the ginger-garlic paste and sauté until the moisture has evaporated and the garlic has had a chance to cook. Add the tomatoes, salt and powdered spices and sauté for six or seven minutes more.

Add the chicken and stir it in the masala (spice paste) for four to five minutes. Pour in enough water to come halfway up the chicken, bring to a boil, then cover and cook over a low heat for 20–30 minutes, or until the chicken is nearly cooked through.

Uncover the pan, increase the flame to high and reduce the liquid in the pan until thick and creamy, stirring often. This will help the sauce become homogenous and deepen its flavours.

Add enough hot water to give a sauce with the consistency of light cream. Taste and adjust the seasoning, stir in the chopped coriander and serve.

serves 6

herby chicken curry

There are many recipes for cooking meats with green herbs in India, this is from the north. Other cooks would add tomatoes and, in the south, they would add fresh coconut or coconut milk as well, so you can change this recipe to reflect your food mood. I find I have started thinking about dishes as being masculine or feminine in nature. This dish has a soft edge, with a perfume of fresh herbs and a delicacy of flavour I feel is rounded and feminine. Men, do not be put off! It might not be robust but is still delicious when you want a light curry. Serve with Chapati or Paratha (see pages 156 and 157), or rice.

Heat 4 tbsp of the oil in a large, non-stick saucepan. Add the onion and cook until well browned. Place all the ingredients for the spice paste into a blender, add the onions and their oil and blend to a fine paste.

Heat the remaining oil in the pan, add the bay leaf and follow after five seconds with the spice paste and chicken joints. Cook, stirring, over a moderate flame for eight to 10 minutes, making sure the paste does not stick to the base of the pan. If it does, add a splash of hot water from the kettle.

Now pour in enough water to cover the chicken by half. Bring to a boil, then cover and place over a low heat until the chicken is cooked through. It should take 20–25 minutes, depending on the size of the chicken joints, and there should be plenty of gorgeous creamy green gravy. If it seems watery, uncover and cook off some of the extra liquid over a high heat, stirring often.

Stir in the garam masala, ground cumin and sour cream; taste. This is when you can balance the dish to perfection by adjusting the salt, lemon juice, garam masala, chilli, or sour cream, as you prefer.

serves 4–6

for the chicken curry
5 tbsp vegetable oil
1 onion, sliced
1 bay leaf
700g small chicken, skinned and jointed
1 good tsp garam masala, or to taste
1 tsp ground cumin
1 tbsp sour cream, or to taste

for the spice paste
100g fresh coriander leaves and stems, washed
1–2 green chillies, stalk removed, or to taste
40g mint leaves, washed
5 large garlic cloves
10g fresh root ginger, peeled weight
2 tsp ground coriander
3 tbsp cashew nuts
3 tbsp lemon juice, or to taste
1 good tsp salt, or to taste

chicken tikka masala

Though everybody 'knows' this dish was invented in Britain, when a diner supposedly wanted sauce with his chicken tikka, its roots are firmly entrenched in one of India's favourite dishes: butter chicken. It is velvety and unapologetically rich. You will need to taste carefully while you cook, as the sweet–sour balance of tomatoes changes with the season and variety. Balance tartness with sugar or cream or, if it is already sweet, omit the sugar. Do not use plum tomatoes; they are too sweet. Serve with Naan or Paratha (see pages 155 and 157).

Mix together all the marinade ingredients with 1 tsp salt. Add the chicken and marinate for as long as possible (overnight, covered, in the fridge is best).

Blend together the ginger and garlic for the curry, using a little water to help. Heat the oil and half the butter in a large non-stick saucepan and add the whole spices. Once they have sizzled for 15 seconds, add the ginger and garlic paste; cook until all the moisture has evaporated and the garlic smells mellow and looks grainy. Add the tomatoes and tomato puree and cook down until the resulting paste releases oil; it should take around 20 minutes. Now brown this paste over gentle heat, stirring often, for six to eight minutes, or until it darkens considerably. Pour in 250ml water, bring to a boil, then pass through a sieve, pressing down to extract as much liquid and flavour as possible from the tomatoes and spices. Discard the solids. Set the sauce aside.

Heat the oven to 240°C, ideally with the grill on too, if your oven can do that. Remove the chicken from the fridge. Place it on a foil-lined baking tray on the uppermost shelf of the oven and cook for eight minutes, or until slightly charred. Remove from the oven. The chicken will finish cooking in the sauce. Cut or pull the meat into large chunks.

Heat the remaining butter and add the green chillies. Add the sauce, salt and a good splash of water and simmer for three or four minutes. Add the chicken, cream, sugar, chilli powder and enough paprika to get a colour you like, then add the powdered fenugreek leaves and garam masala. Simmer, stirring often, for four or five minutes, or until the chicken is done and the sauce is lovely and creamy. You may need to add a little more water. Taste and adjust the balance to your palate by adding more salt, sugar or cream. Sprinkle over the coriander leaves and serve.

serves 4

for the tikka marinade
3–4 tsp lemon juice, depending on the tartness of the yogurt
110g Greek yogurt
2 fat garlic cloves, grated into a paste
10g fresh root ginger, peeled weight, grated into a paste
¼–½ tsp chilli powder
1½ tsp paprika powder, for colour (optional)
1½ tsp ground cumin
2 tbsp vegetable oil

for the curry
6 boneless chicken thighs
20g fresh root ginger, peeled weight
8 garlic cloves
2 tbsp vegetable oil
80g butter
1 black cardamom pod
6 green cardamom pods
2cm cinnamon stick
4 cloves
500g vine tomatoes, blended to a fine puree
1 tbsp tomato puree
2–4 small green chillies, whole but pierced
salt, to taste
80–100ml single cream, or to taste
1 tsp sugar, or to taste
¼–½ tsp chilli powder
1 tsp paprika powder, or to taste
1 rounded tsp dried fenugreek leaves, crushed to a powder
1 tsp garam masala
small handful of fresh coriander leaves, to serve

chicken and vegetables in an aromatic coconut sauce

This is a beautiful, full-flavoured, creamy dish that hails from the Christians of Kerala. It is known as *ishtu*, a word that is a derivation of 'stew', because this is a naturally-fused dish of east and west. Chicken and vegetables are all cooked together with the local flavours of the south western coast of India. There are lots of spices, but the flavours have been mellowed by coconut. Don't worry, you can still taste lovely bits of ginger and the flavours of star anise and fennel seeds. You can make this without vegetables, or add whatever vegetables you have in the fridge; it's that kind of dish. Lovely with rice, Naan or Paratha (see pages 155 and 157), or even the rice noodles which are often eaten in Kerala.

Heat the oil in a wide pan (a karahi or wok is ideal). Add the whole spices and, once the seeds have stopped popping, the curry leaves. Follow immediately with the onion and cook over a moderate heat until translucent. Add the ginger, garlic and green chillies and sauté gently for one or two minutes, or until the garlic is cooked.

Add the turmeric, chilli, ground coriander, fennel seeds and salt with a splash of water and cook for two minutes. Put in the chicken and cook in the spice paste for two minutes more. Pour in water to come one-third of the way up the chicken, bring to a boil, then lower the flame and cook, covered, for 20 minutes, stirring occasionally. The liquid in the pot should have reduced quite a bit by now. Add most of the coconut milk (try and add only the thin milk that collects at the bottom of the can at this point), cover and cook for another five minutes. Uncover and cook off most of the excess liquid, giving the pan occasional stirs. Check the chicken is cooked all the way through, with no trace of pink.

Stir in the remaining thick coconut milk, coconut cream (if using), tamarind, beans and peas; the dish should be creamy. Taste and adjust the seasoning. Simmer for three to four minutes, then serve with the coriander leaves.

serves 4–6

6 tbsp coconut or vegetable oil
1 tsp mustard seeds
5cm cinnamon stick
6 green cardamom pods
4 cloves
10 black peppercorns
2 star anise
15 curry leaves
1 onion, finely sliced
20g fresh root ginger, peeled weight, finely chopped
6 garlic cloves, finely chopped
2–4 green chillies, whole but pierced
½ tsp turmeric
¼–½ tsp chilli powder
1 tbsp ground coriander
2 tsp fennel seeds, roughly powdered
salt, to taste
500g skinless chicken joints
400ml can coconut milk
1 tbsp coconut cream (optional)
¾–1 tsp tamarind paste, or to taste
handful of green beans, topped and tailed, halved on the diagonal
2 handfuls of green peas, fresh or frozen and defrosted
small fistful of fresh coriander leaves

spicy andhra chicken curry

Andhra is a region known for its great hot food and this dish is just that, bold and absolutely wonderful. Although it might look complicated, it's actually quite easy to cook and, as it uses boneless chicken, all comes together quite quickly. The chicken would normally be deep-fried before being added to the sauce, but I don't do that. It's up to you. If the dish seems too spicy, add a little milk, single cream or coconut milk to tame the flavours. White poppy seeds have a lovely taste and creaminess, you can make it without them but I recommend you seek them out as they are a fantastic store cupboard ingredient. This is great with rice and Indian breads.

Using a mortar and pestle, or a spice grinder, grind together the whole spices and chillies to a fine powder. Separately blend together the ginger and garlic to a fine paste, adding a little water to help. Take around one-third of this paste and mix it with the marinade ingredients, adding ¼ tsp of salt. Add to the chicken, mix well and marinate for as long as possible, up to overnight in the refrigerator, though even 30 minutes will help.

Heat the oil in a non-stick saucepan. Add the onion and sauté until golden brown. Add the remaining ginger-garlic paste and cook until the water has evaporated, then continute to cook gently until the garlic is colouring. Add the tomatoes and curry leaves and cook for six to eight minutes over high heat until the oil is released on the sides of the pan; stir more as it thickens.

Add the ground whole spices, cumin, coriander, salt and a good splash of water. Cook until the pan dries out, stirring often. Add another splash of water and repeat. By now the sauce should be cooked and homogenous.

Add the chicken and its marinade. Continue cooking over a high heat, stirring constantly until the yogurt has been incorporated. Add 150ml water, bring to a boil and cook until the chicken is done (around five minutes for breast and eight for thighs). Stir often, as it will help bring the sauce to a lovely creamy consistency. Taste and adjust the seasoning to your taste; you may want more chilli powder or lemon juice.

serves 4

for the curry
1 tbsp white poppy seeds
6 cloves
1cm cinnamon stick
½ tsp black peppercorns or ground black pepper
2 tsp fennel seeds
3–6 dried red chillies, seeds shaken out if you prefer
20g fresh root ginger, peeled weight
6 fat garlic cloves
salt, to taste
400g boneless, skinless chicken thighs or breast, in 5cm pieces
5–6 tbsp vegetable oil
1 onion, finely chopped
2 smallish tomatoes, blended to a smooth puree
14 fresh curry leaves
½ tsp ground cumin
2 tsp ground coriander

for the marinade
½ tsp turmeric
½ tsp chilli powder, or to taste
2 heaped tbsp yogurt
2 tsp lemon juice, or to taste

chilli chicken balti

Many curryphiles have argued over the roots of balti, but I don't think there has been a general consensus. What I do know is that Birmingham is known for its baltis, rich tomato- and yogurt-based curries that can contain almost anything. This is my chicken balti, with lots of green chillies as much for their flavour as heat. They really add to the dish and I do recommend you leave them in. I'm not sure it will taste quite the same as the balti in your favourite curry house, but it is delicious nonetheless.

15g fresh root ginger, peeled weight
6 fat garlic cloves
2 largish tomatoes, quartered
1½ tsp garam masala
1½ tsp ground cumin
1 tbsp ground coriander
½ tsp turmeric
1 tsp paprika, for colour
1 rounded tbsp full-fat yogurt
salt, to taste
6 tbsp vegetable oil
¾ tsp brown mustard seeds
1 bay leaf
1 onion, finely chopped
6–10 green chillies, whole but
  pierced
500g boneless chicken thighs, cut
  into 2.5–5cm pieces
lots of freshly ground black pepper
1 tbsp lemon juice, or to taste
large handful of finely chopped fresh
  coriander leaves and stems

Blend together the ginger, garlic and tomatoes until smooth. Stir in the ground spices, yogurt and ¾ tsp salt.

Heat the oil in a non-stick saucepan. Add the mustard seeds and cook until they have popped. Add the bay leaf, onion and green chillies and cook over a moderate flame, stirring often, for six to eight minutes, until the onions are well browned.

Add the blended ingredients and cook on a high flame, stirring constantly, until the mixture comes to a boil and most of the excess liquid in the pan has evaporated. Continue cooking, stirring often, until the paste releases oil.

Add the chicken and stir it in the thick masala for a few minutes. Add enough water to come halfway up the chicken. Bring back to a boil and cook for seven minutes.

Increase the heat and toss the chicken in the sauce for another five minutes; the sauce will reduce to a lovely creamy consistency. Check a piece of chicken by cutting through; there should be no pink in the middle. Adjust the consistency of the sauce by adding a little water or reducing it a little further, as you prefer.

Taste and adjust the seasoning to your liking, adding lots of black pepper and a little lemon juice if your sauce is not tart enough. Stir in the chopped coriander and serve.

serves 4–5, can be halved

creamy almond chicken curry

A fabulous creamy, nutty dish that is great for the family and for friends. I like to use small chickens as I find them more succulent, and keep the bones in for that delicious flavour. If you don't like the bones you can just cook thigh fillets, the dish will still work. If your yogurt is particularly sour, add only 160-180g. I like to top the dish with lightly fried and halved almonds, or fried brown, crisp onions.

600g small skinless chicken joints (see recipe introduction)
200g plain, full-fat yogurt
25g fresh root ginger, peeled weight, grated into a paste
5 fat garlic cloves, grated into a paste
salt, to taste
5 tbsp ghee or vegetable oil
2 bay leaves
1 onion, finely chopped
25g blanched almonds (see page 36)
2–4 green chillies, whole but pierced, or to taste
5 rounded tbsp ground almonds
½ tsp ground, sifted green cardamom seeds
1 tsp ground cumin, or to taste
1 tsp garam masala, or to taste
¾ tsp finely ground black pepper, or to taste
80–100ml single cream
handful of chopped fresh coriander

Marinade the chicken in the yogurt, ginger and garlic with 1 tsp salt for as long as possible; even 20 minutes if that is all you have, though you can leave it overnight in the fridge.

Heat 4 tbsp of the ghee or oil in a non-stick saucepan. Add the bay leaves and onion and gently fry until translucent and really soft. Add the chicken and cook over a highish flame, stirring and turning the chicken in the yogurt constantly, until it comes to a boil. Continue to cook and stir for five minutes further. Now cook, stirring often but not constantly, until the yogurt has reduced considerably and you can see the fat being released at the base of the pan. It should take another 10 minutes or so. Taste, it should be well-balanced and the garlic should be cooked.

Pour in enough water to cover the chicken by half, bring to a boil, cover and simmer over a gentle flame for 10–20 minutes, or until the chicken is ready. The time it takes will depend on the size of the chicken joints and how long it took to reduce the yogurt. Give the pot an occasional stir and make sure it does not run dry. Check the chicken is done by cutting into a thick piece; there should be no trace of pink.

Meanwhile, heat the remaining 1 tbsp ghee or oil in a small saucepan. Add the almonds and fry over a medium-low heat until lightly toasted and golden. Drain on kitchen paper, split in half where the natural crease is, and set aside.

Stir the remaining ingredients into the chicken, then pour in enough water to get a sauce the consistency of double cream. Taste; this is the time to balance the flavours by adding a little more cumin, black pepper or garam masala, as you prefer. Sprinkle over the almonds and serve.

serves 4–5

cardamom-scented chicken curry

This is a really light, almost broth-like curry from the Sindhi community. It is like chicken soup: soul food, comfort food, home food and what you want to eat when you feel poorly. You can eat it like a soup with buttered crusty bread, or with plain boiled rice. Cardamom can differ in strength, so I leave it to you to decide how much to add; you can always put in more at the end of cooking, if you want.

4 tbsp vegetable oil
1 onion, finely chopped
15g fresh root ginger, peeled weight, grated into a paste
4 fat garlic cloves, grated into a paste
1 tomato, chopped
2–3 green chillies, whole but pierced
⅔–¾ tsp ground cardamom seeds, or to taste
1 rounded tsp ground coriander
¾ tsp ground cumin
⅓–½ tsp freshly ground black pepper, or to taste
salt, to taste
450g skinless chicken joints
1 rounded tsp cornflour
handful of chopped fresh coriander

Heat the oil in a non-stick saucepan. Add the onion and sauté until well browned. Add the ginger and garlic pastes and cook, stirring, for a minute or two, until the garlic is cooked and starting to colour.

Add the tomato, chillies, powdered spices and salt. Sauté for a few minutes, then add a splash of water and cook for six or seven minutes more, until the oil begins to come out of the masala, stirring more as the mixture dries up.

Add the chicken and sauté and brown in the masala for a few minutes; it will start to stick to the base of the pan. Add 400ml water, bring to a boil, cover and simmer until the chicken is cooked. It will take 25–35 minutes, depending on the size of the joints.

Stir a little water into the cornflour so that it dissolves, stir this into the chicken and cook for another few minutes. Add extra water to the pan if necessary; the sauce should be light and thin. Stir in the chopped coriander, taste and adjust with more black pepper or cardamom, to taste, then serve.

serves 4

chicken coconut masala

This is a spicy, full-bodied curry from the region of Andhra, known for its hot food and red chillies, with both tomatoes and tamarind adding a tang. The sweet flecks of fresh coconut hidden inside both soften the spices and add a lovely texture. If you don't have fresh coconut, add a little coconut cream; you will not have the same texture but it will still taste delicious. Serve with wholewheat Indian breads, such as Chapati or Paratha (see pages 156 and 157).

Place the whole spices in a small saucepan and dry roast until the coriander seeds are lightly coloured. Grind to a fine powder.

Heat the oil in a pan and fry the onion until brown. Add the ginger and garlic pastes and fry gently for a couple of minutes, until the garlic smells cooked. Add all the spices and salt, stir for 20 seconds, add a small splash of water and cook for two minutes more. Now tip in the tomatoes and chicken and sauté over a medium-high flame for seven or eight minutes, or until the sauce has been absorbed by the chicken. Add enough water to come halfway up the chicken, bring to a boil, then cover and simmer gently for 25–35 minutes, or until done, depending on the size of the joints. Stir occasionally and make sure there is enough water in the pan.

Once the chicken is cooked, add the tamarind paste and coconut and cook for a further three or four minutes. The sauce should be quite thick; if it isn't, cook for a little longer on a high flame. Taste and adjust the seasoning and tamarind to taste, and serve sprinkled with chopped coriander.

serves 4–5

1½ tsp fennel seeds
4–6 dried red chillies, seeds shaken out
⅔ tsp black peppercorns
2.5cm cinnamon stick
4 cloves
4 green cardamom pods, whole
1½ tsp coriander seeds
6 tbsp vegetable oil
1 onion, finely chopped
15g ginger, peeled weight, grated into a paste
4 fat garlic cloves, grated into a paste
salt, to taste
2½ tomatoes (not sweet), quartered and blended or chopped
600g skinless chicken joints
½–⅔ tsp tamarind paste, or to taste
50–60g grated fresh coconut, or 30g creamed coconut (the latter will be sweeter)
handful of fresh coriander leaves, chopped

golden chicken korma

A lovely dish, creamy and nutty with the clear flavours of whole spices. Korma was not always a Friday night special. It started life in palaces and was eaten by kings, so while I've added turmeric here, I prefer to give this dish the respect it deserves and use a good pinch of saffron (infuse it in 2 tbsp hot milk as you cook, and add it at the end), though the budget can't always stretch to that! If you're feeling flush, finish with a little edible gold leaf on top. The white poppy seeds are one of those secret ingredients that will make your korma special.

Blend the ginger and garlic with a little water to help make a smooth paste. Separately blend the cashew nuts with enough water to cover, to make another smooth paste. Set both aside.

Heat the oil in a large, wide non-stick saucepan. Add the whole spices and bay leaves and allow to sizzle for 10–20 seconds. Add the onion and cook gently until really soft but not coloured. Add the ginger-garlic paste and continue to cook until the liquid has dried up and the garlic smells cooked and is lightly golden.

Add the chicken, yogurt, coriander, turmeric and salt. Cook, stirring and folding the chicken in the yogurt constantly, until it comes to a boil. Then continue cooking until the yogurt has been absorbed by the chicken. Add enough water to come halfway up the chicken, bring back to a boil, then reduce the heat to low, cover and cook gently for 20–30 minutes, giving the pot an occasional stir. The chicken should be nearly done.

Check the pot after 20 minutes and, if there is a lot of liquid, finish cooking the chicken over a high heat, uncovered so the excess cooks off. The sauce should be creamy.

Once the chicken is done, add the ground almonds, cashew nut paste, cream, poppy seeds and coconut. Simmer for five minutes, or until the sauce has the right creamy consistency. Add lemon juice to taste and adjust the seasonings. Serve topped with any one - or even several - of the options given, to finish the dish.

serves 4–5

for the korma
25g fresh root ginger, peeled weight
5 fat garlic cloves
40g cashew nuts
4 tbsp vegetable oil
1 tsp caraway seeds
7.5cm cinnamon stick
6 cloves
2 blades mace
10 green cardamom pods
10 black peppercorns
2 bay leaves
1 onion, finely chopped
600g chicken, skinned and jointed
    (I prefer small chickens)
160g plain yogurt
1 rounded tsp ground coriander
⅓ tsp turmeric
salt, to taste
3 tbsp ground almonds
4 tbsp double cream
1 tbsp white poppy seeds (optional
    but special)
30–40g block creamed coconut, or
    2–3 tbsp coconut cream
1–2 tsp lemon juice

to finish
Choose from quartered dried figs,
    raisins, toasted flaked almonds,
    roasted cashews, hazelnuts or
    pistachios, saffron, fried fresh root
    ginger julienne, edible gold leaf

light cumin-flavoured chicken curry

A simple, delicious curry that's one of my favourites, and a lovely platform for the humble cumin seed to shine. The flavours are simple, so the chicken should be on the bone for maximum taste. Ideally, serve with Chapati (see page 156).

Blend together the yogurt, ginger and garlic until smooth. Stir in the ground cumin and coriander, ¾ tsp salt and the black pepper. Pour this marinade over the chicken and leave for as long as you can, even 20 minutes will help, or up to one day, covered, in the refrigerator.

Heat the oil in a non-stick saucepan. Add the cumin seeds and, once they have darkened, add the onions and fry until golden brown. Add the chicken, its marinade, the chillies and garam masala and cook over a medium-high flame, stirring often, until the yogurt comes to a boil and then gets absorbed by the chicken. Pour in enough water to come halfway up the chicken and bring back to a boil.

Cover and simmer over a gentle flame for 20–30 minutes, until the chicken is nearly done (20 minutes for a small chicken, 30 minutes for a medium chicken). Check occasionally and give the pot a stir.

Uncover the pan and reduce the liquid until it is quite thick and creamy; this will deepen the flavour. Add a splash of water if you need to, you want to achieve a thick, creamy sauce. Taste and adjust the seasoning, stir in the chopped coriander and serve.

serves 4–5

150g plain yogurt
20g fresh root ginger, peeled weight
6 fat garlic cloves
2 tsp ground cumin
2 tsp ground coriander
salt, to taste
¼ tsp freshly ground black pepper
600g small skinless chicken joints
4–5 tbsp vegetable oil
1 rounded tsp cumin seeds
2 small onions, finely chopped
2–5 green chillies, whole but pierced
1 tsp garam masala
handful of chopped fresh coriander

parsi-style duck with apricots

Inspired by a chicken dish, but I love these sweet, sour and fruity flavours with duck. The Parsis were originally from Persia, but their food is a fascinating story of their Indian journey. They adopted the sweet flavours of Gujarat, where many of them first lived, but also of the Raj, as they considered themselves quite western. They employed some of India's best chefs who were - at the time - from Goa. This recipe combines all these influences. It's always served with a tangle of fine, straw-like fried potatoes, which add a lovely crunch.

15g fresh root ginger, peeled weight
5 garlic cloves
4–6 dried Kashmiri chillies, seeds shaken out
1½ tsp cumin seeds
1½ tsp coriander seeds
14 black peppercorns
6 cloves
seeds from 6 green cardamom pods
5 tbsp vegetable oil
4cm cinnamon stick
2 onions, chopped
salt, to taste
500g duck legs and thighs, skinned and jointed
4 largish tomatoes, finely chopped
14 dried, ready-to-eat apricots
1½-2 tsp grated jaggery, or sugar, or to taste
2 tsp white wine vinegar, or to taste

Make a paste of the ginger and garlic, using a little water to help. Using a spice blender or mortar and pestle, make a fine powder of the dried chillies, cumin and coriander seeds, peppercorns, cloves and cardamom.

Heat the oil in a large non-stick saucepan. Add the cinnamon and onions and fry until well browned. Add the ginger and garlic pastes and cook for a couple of minutes, until golden and the garlic smells cooked. Tip in the powdered spices and salt with a good splash of water and cook for two minutes. Add the duck and tomatoes and stir for a few minutes, then pour in enough water to just cover, bring to a boil, cover and cook gently for 40 minutes, stirring occasionally. You shouldn't need more water, but add a little if the pan is dry.

Add the apricots, jaggery or sugar, vinegar and a splash of water if the pan looks a little too dry; cover and cook for another 10 minutes. The sauce should now be quite thick and the duck will be tender. Taste and adjust the balance of sour and sweet flavours, adding vinegar or sugar to your taste. Serve with the potato straws below.

serves 4

for the potato straws (*salli*)

Toss the potato straws in the salt in a bowl. Gently heat 4cm oil in a saucepan (the wider the pan the more you can cook at once). Once the oil is medium hot, squeeze out as much water as you can from the potatoes and add a couple of large handfuls to the oil. (Do not overcrowd the pan.)

Fry for five to six minutes, breaking up any tangles as much as you can with a spoon, until lightly golden and crisp. Remove with a slotted spoon and drain on kitchen paper. Repeat until you have cooked all the straws.

400g potatoes, finely shredded (I use the slicer part of my box grater, then finely slice the paper-thin potato rounds into long, fine julienne, it works beautifully)·
½ tsp salt
vegetable oil, to deep-fry

tamarind duck curry

This is a lovely, deep, tangy dish that is great with or without coconut milk. Without the coconut, the flavours are clear and deep. The coconut adds sweetness to this Keralan recipe and is authentic. I leave it to you; taste before adding the coconut and decide. Balance the tamarind accordingly, the coconut version requires more tartness, as well as salt. I have tried this with duck breasts but it doesn't work nearly as well. If you hate bones, I still urge you to keep them in and take a few minutes at the end to pick the meat from the bones and stir it back in.

Using a good mortar and pestle, pound the green cardamom, cloves and black peppercorns together to a fine powder, removing the green cardamom skin. Separately blend together the ginger and garlic with a little water until smooth.

Heat the oil in a non-stick saucepan. Add the cinnamon and onions and cook until well browned. Add the ginger-garlic paste and cook until the excess water has dried up and the garlic has had a chance to fry and smells cooked. Add all the powdered spices and salt along with a small splash of water and cook for two minutes.

Add the duck and stir well in the masala; start to brown the duck, then add the chillies (if using). Pour in enough water to just cover, bring to a boil, cover the pan, reduce the heat and simmer gently for 50–60 minutes, until the duck is tender; stir occasionally and check there is some liquid in the pan. After 45 minutes, check to see how much liquid remains; if it is more than halfway up the duck, finish cooking the duck uncovered so the excess water cooks off.

At this time, heat the oil for the tarka in a small pan. Add the mustard seeds and, once they have popped, the curry leaves. Follow with the onion and cook until well browned. Add to the duck with the coconut milk (if using) and tamarind, then simmer for five minutes. Taste, adjust the seasoning, adding more tamarind if you would prefer a tangier dish, then serve.

serves 4

for the curry
12 green cardamom pods
6 cloves
12 black peppercorns
30g fresh root ginger, peeled weight
9 garlic cloves
6 tbsp vegetable oil
5cm cinnamon stick
3 small onions, sliced
1 rounded tbsp ground coriander
¾ tsp turmeric
½ tsp chilli powder
salt, to taste
600g duck joints (I buy 3 whole duck legs and joint them into thighs and drumsticks, leave the skin on or not, as you prefer)
3–6 green chillies, whole but pierced (optional)
150–200ml coconut milk (optional, see recipe introduction)
1–1½ tsp tamarind paste, or to taste

for the tarka
1 tbsp vegetable oil
¾ tsp mustard seeds
15 fresh curry leaves
1 small onion, chopped

meat

lamb and spinach curry

This is delicious and so much better than the sum of its parts, another of the dishes from my childhood. When I wanted to write this recipe, I only had a vague memory of what went in it, so I spent days in my kitchen getting the balance right until it was good enough to remind me of home. I finally got there and it is as sublime as I remember. It does take a while to cook, but involves minimal preparation and is not difficult to make. Serve with Chapati (see page 156) and nothing else. Whole leaf spinach has more flavour and I use the roots too, if there are any. Baby spinach tastes lighter and more velvety so, if you choose that, increase the quantity to 400g.

30g fresh root ginger, peeled weight
3 tomatoes, quartered
6 large garlic cloves
6 tbsp vegetable oil
2 black cardamom pods
4 cloves
5cm cinnamon stick
2 bay leaves
1 onion, finely chopped
salt, to taste
2 tbsp ground coriander
¾ tsp turmeric
¾ tsp ground cumin
¼–½ tsp chilli powder, or to taste
600g leg of lamb, with bones, cubed
  by the butcher, or 500g boneless
  lamb, cubed
1–3 green chillies, whole but pierced
  (optional)
300–350g spinach, well washed
1 rounded tsp garam masala

Finely slice 20g of the ginger into matchsticks and set aside. Blend the rest of the ginger with the tomatoes, garlic and a splash of water until smooth.

Heat 5½ tbsp oil in a large non-stick saucepan, add the whole spices and bay leaves and follow 15 seconds later with the onion. Cook the onion until deep golden. Add the tomato paste, salt, coriander, turmeric, cumin and chilli powder and cook over a moderate flame until it becomes a paste and releases droplets of oil on the base of a pan; it should take 15-20 minutes. Reduce the heat and sauté the paste for another five to seven minutes, stirring.

Add the lamb and a splash of water, then sauté the meat and paste over a moderate flame for five or six minutes, until the paste has been completely absorbed by the lamb. Pour in enough water to cover, bring to a boil, then reduce the heat to low, cover and simmer gently for 50–60 minutes, or until the lamb is tender. The sauce should only come one-quarter of the way up the lamb. If necessary, reduce some of the liquid over a high heat.

Heat the remaining oil in a saucepan, add the ginger julienne and green chillies (if using); cook for a minute, then remove both with a slotted spoon. Add the spinach and a splash of water to the empty saucepan and cook until completely wilted. At this stage, you can blend the spinach to a smooth paste or leave it whole. Add to the lamb with the garam masala, ginger julienne and chillies, cover and simmer for another four minutes. Taste, adjust the seasoning and serve.

serves 4–5

authentic pork vindaloo

I have tried the vindaloo served in some British curry houses and I'm sorry to say it is mostly an amalgamation of those restaurants' different curry sauces with lots of chillies, with no real Goan flavour. Those curries have little to do with real vindaloo... except that they are hot. An authentic vindaloo does use a fair amount of chillies, but that's not its defining feature. It has wonderful spices, vinegar, ginger and garlic to bring the best out of the rich pork, and doesn't have the thick sauce of curry house versions. This is a true vindaloo, with a light liquor. For the best flavour, cook the pork in minimal water so it stews, as much as possible, in its own juices. I quite like it with sautéed potatoes to soak up the lovely sauce. This is my version, learnt from a Goan, and but I have lightened up on the number of chillies he would use.

Using a spice grinder, grind the whole spices and chillies to a fine powder.

Make a paste of the ginger, garlic and vinegar. Add this to the pork along with the spices and salt, cover and marinate in the fridge for a couple of hours, if you have time.

Heat the oil in a non-stick saucepan. Add the onion and fry until golden brown. Add the pork and marinade and brown gently over a moderate heat for six or seven minutes. Reduce the heat to low, cover and cook for 40–50 minutes, or until the pork is tender, checking every so often and adding a splash of water from the kettle if the pot looks like it is running dry.

Once the pork is tender, taste, adjust the seasoning and serve. Some people like to add a little sugar. I don't, but I leave it to you to decide.

serves 4

1 tsp cumin seeds
1 tsp coriander seeds
5–10 dried red Kashmiri chillies
   (or 3–6 hotter dried red chillies),
   halved, seeds shaken out
6 black peppercorns
3 green cardamom pods
4 cloves
2cm cinnamon stick
13g ginger, peeled weight, roughly
   chopped
7 fat garlic cloves
3 tbsp good-quality white wine
   vinegar, or to taste
400g pork shoulder with some fat, in
   2.5cm cubes
50g belly of pork, in 2.5cm pieces
salt, to taste
4 tbsp vegetable oil
1 small onion, finely chopped
sugar, to taste

tangy lamb chops with dried pomegranate

I love this dish and cook it when I have people over and want to wow them, as it's delicious and different but also really easy. The main flavour is the dried pomegranate powder, which you can buy in Asian stores or on the internet. It comes from the seeds of a very different variety of fruit from that we are used to eating; the flavours are really distinctive and tangy rather than sweet. The sauce clings to the meat with a little extra left to mop up with flatbread. For the best flavour, make this recipe with spring lamb chops. Serve with a vegetable dish or simply a raita (see pages 169-171) and Indian flatbread.

Heat the oil in a large non-stick saucepan. Add the onions and fry for six to eight minutes, until well browned.

Meanwhile, make a fine paste of the ginger and garlic with the help of a little water. Add to the cooked onions, cook off the excess moisture, then gently fry the paste for another minute.

Add the lamb and brown well. Add the spices, chillies, salt and a splash of water. Cook over a moderate flame, stirring often until the pan is dry again. Add 200ml water, bring to a boil, then cover the pan and cook gently until the lamb is done; it should take 30–35 minutes. Stir occasionally and check to see there is enough water in the pan.

Once the lamb is cooked, reduce any leftover sauce until it is quite thick. Taste and adjust the seasoning, adding a little more dried pomegranate powder if you feel it needs more of that lovely, fruity tartness. Stir in the chopped coriander and pomegranate seeds and serve.

serves 4

6 tbsp vegetable oil
2 small onions, finely chopped
20g fresh root ginger, peeled weight
6 fat garlic cloves
650g (around 8) lamb chops,
    trimmed of excess fat
1 tsp garam masala
1½ tsp ground coriander
3 tsp dried pomegranate powder
    (*anardana*), or to taste
2–4 green chillies, whole but pierced,
    or to taste
salt, to taste
handful of chopped fresh coriander
    leaves
handful of fresh pomegranate seeds

beef madras

A firm British favourite, this is rich in flavour, spicy and comforting. A madras is normally a hot curry; for a medium heat I add four dried Kashmiri chillies and two green chillies, so bear this in mind and add as many as you think you will like. Kashmiri chillies are mild with an amazing deep red colour and can be found in well-stocked supermarkets. If you can't find them, add chilli powder to taste instead. Serve with pilaf, Naan (see page 155) or Indian flatbreads.

Using a spice grinder, grind all the whole spices and chillies to a fine powder.

Heat the oil in a large non-stick saucepan. Add the onion and cook until well browned. Stir in all the spices, salt and a splash of water and cook for one minute.

Add the beef and brown in the spice paste for a good six to eight minutes over a moderate heat. I often add a splash of water when it starts to stick.

Meanwhile, blend the ginger, garlic and tomatoes until smooth, using a little water to help. Add to the pan with the green chillies, bring to a boil, then cover and simmer gently until the liquid has reduced. Check after 10 minutes, give the pot a stir and come back in another five minutes.

Now increase the heat and brown the beef and sauce together until it has been absorbed by the beef. Pour in enough water to cover, bring back to a boil, cover and cook until the meat is tender; it will take around 1¼ hours.

Uncover the lid and reduce the sauce in the pan until it is creamy. Add the cream and chopped coriander, taste, adjust the seasoning and serve.

serves 4

2.5cm cinnamon stick
10 green cardamom pods
8 cloves
10 black peppercorns
2 tsp cumin seeds
1 tbsp coriander seeds
3–6 dried Kashmiri red chillies, seeds shaken out
5 tbsp vegetable oil
1 onion, sliced
½ tsp turmeric
1–1¼ tsp garam masala, or to taste
salt, to taste
500g diced beef
20g fresh root ginger, peeled weight
7 garlic cloves
2 tomatoes
2–5 green chillies, whole but pierced (optional)
4 tbsp single cream
handful of chopped fresh coriander

rich lamb shank curry

An absolutely delicious, meaty feast that is the perfect dish for a dinner party. The lamb shanks look so dramatic on the plate and people know you have made an effort. It is not difficult to make and, though it takes a little patience, it's worth it. The sauce is rich and deep in flavour and works with Indian breads or with rice.

Blend the tomatoes, ginger and garlic until smooth.

Heat the oil in a large saucepan. Brown the lamb shanks in the oil for two or three minutes, getting a little colour on all sides. Remove and set aside.

Reheat the oil, add the whole spices and bay leaves and, after 20 seconds, the onion; cook until the onion is well browned. Add the lamb, blended tomatoes, cumin, chilli powder, ground coriander, green chillies and salt; bring to a boil. Cover and cook over a low heat, stirring occasionally, until you have a little less than half the liquid you started with; it should take 15–20 minutes.

Now increase the heat and brown the meat and sauce, stirring very often, until the oil comes out of the sauce and it has reduced considerably. This really intensifies the flavours.

Add enough water to just cover the lamb shanks, bring to a boil, cover and cook over a gentle flame for 1–1¼ hours, or until the lamb is tender and done to your liking. Stir every 10–15 minutes and turn the meat in the sauce. Add a splash of hot water if the pan looks like it is running dry.

When the lamb is tender and coming off the bone, reduce any excess liquid in the pan over a high heat until you have a creamy sauce. Taste and adjust the seasoning, stir in the garam masala and herbs and serve.

serves 4

2 large tomatoes, quartered
15g fresh root ginger, peeled weight
6 fat garlic cloves
6 tbsp vegetable oil
4 x 400–500g lamb shanks
20 black peppercorns
5 cloves
2.5cm cinnamon stick
4 green cardamom pods
2 black cardamom pods
2 bay leaves
1 largish onion, chopped
1 good tsp ground cumin
¼–½ tsp chilli powder for heat,
    or paprika powder for colour
    (optional)
2 tsp ground coriander
2–4 green chillies (preferably Indian
    green finger), whole but pierced
salt, to taste
1 tsp garam masala
handful of fresh coriander and/or a
    few shredded mint leaves

hearty meatball and pea curry

Meatballs in the west are known as hearty home-style food. But in India, meatballs - or koftas as they are known - are so loved that they have been refined to restaurant fare, stuffed with nuts or raisins and finished with cream. This sauce has a light, creamy consistency that coats all the grains of fluffy white basmati rice with which it should be served. The fresh coriander is more than a decoration here, it really lifts the deep, earthy flavours of the meat.

Mix together all the ingredients for the meatballs until really well combined - your hands are the best tool for this - and set aside. Start the sauce by blending together the tomatoes, ginger and garlic until smooth.

Heat the oil in a large saucepan. Add the whole spices and bay leaves and cook for 20 seconds. Now add the onion and cook until golden brown. Add the blended tomatoes, powdered spices and salt and cook down until it is a thick paste that starts to release oil on the sides of the pan. Cook further, stirring constantly, for a few more minutes to deepen the flavours.

Add 700ml water and bring to a boil. Check the seasoning. Make walnut-sized meatballs from the minced meat mixture and pop each into the simmering curry (I get 20 meatballs). Simmer, covered, for 10 minutes, then add the peas, bring back to a simmer and cook for another five minutes.

Uncover; the sauce should have reduced to a light creamy consistency. If not, take out the meatballs and boil over a high heat until it is. Check the seasoning, shake in the chopped coriander and serve.

serves 4–6

for the meatballs
400g minced beef or lamb
2 large slices of white bread, crusts removed, made into breadcrumbs
1 egg, beaten
¾ tsp salt
½ tsp garam masala
5g fresh root ginger, peeled weight, grated into a paste
1 fat garlic clove, grated into a paste

for the sauce
3 tomatoes
20g fresh root ginger, peeled weight
5 fat garlic cloves
6 tbsp vegetable oil
6 green cardamom pods
6 cloves
2.5cm cinnamon stick
1 blade mace
2 bay leaves
1 onion, finely chopped
2 tsp ground coriander
¼–¾ tsp chilli powder, to taste
1 rounded tsp garam masala
½ tsp ground cumin
salt, to taste
2 handfuls of peas
large handful of chopped fresh coriander

lamb do piaza

A much-loved British dish that's also a favourite in India. It is, at heart, a richly flavoured mutton or goat curry with double the amount of onions normally used. This is a great recipe to prepare a day in advance of serving, as the beautiful tangle of flavours continue to soften and marry. If you can add some lamb bones (ask your butcher), you'll get an added depth of flavour. For a wow factor, deep-fry some more finely sliced onions until crispy and pile a dramatic mound of them on top.

Heat the oil in a non-stick saucepan. Add the whole spices and, once they have sizzled a bit, add the chopped onions and cook until browned; the darker the onion, the deeper the flavour.

Meanwhile, make a fine paste of the tomatoes, ginger and garlic using a hand blender. Stir in the powdered spices, salt and yogurt until smooth.

Add the lamb to the pan and seal the outsides. Add the tomato-yogurt paste and bring to a boil while stirring very often. Then reduce the heat, cover and cook for 45–50 minutes, or until the lamb is tender. Add the sliced onions 30 minutes into the cooking process and give the pot a stir every 10–15 minutes, making sure it does not dry out. Ideally, the dish should cook in its own sauce but, if necessary, add a splash of water.

By the time the lamb is tender, the sauce should have reduced to a creamy consistency with a tangle of sweet, sliced onions. If it is too dry, add a splash of water. Taste and add more salt, chilli powder or lemon juice, as you prefer, until it is perfect for you. Stir in the chopped coriander and serve with Paratha, Chapati or Naan (see pages 155–157).

serves 4–6

4–5 tbsp vegetable oil (use 5 tbsp if your lamb is quite lean)
3 green cardamom pods
2.5cm cinnamon stick
4 cloves
8 black peppercorns
2 smallish onions, 1½ chopped and ½ sliced
2 large tomatoes, quartered
10g fresh root ginger, peeled weight
5 large garlic cloves
½ tsp turmeric
1 tsp ground cumin
1½ tsp ground coriander
1 tsp garam masala
¼–½ tsp chilli powder, or to taste (add some paprika for colour if you don't use much)
salt, to taste
4 tbsp Greek yogurt
500g leg of lamb, cubed
lemon juice, to taste
good handful of chopped fresh coriander leaves

keralan pork curry

This delicious recipe must come from the Christians of Kerala. It is not too spicy and has a lovely blend of flavours, with a hint of fruitiness from the raisins that really complements pork. I like to sprinkle the finished dish with grated coconut, which you fold in when you serve yourself, but if you don't have any the curry is just as good without it. You can find frozen grated coconut in Asian stores; it's a great freezer staple. Serve with rice or Paratha (see page 157).

Using a good mortar and pestle, pound the mustard seeds, cinnamon and cloves until fine. Separately blend together the garlic, ginger and raisins with a small splash of water until smooth.

Heat the oil in a large non-stick saucepan. Add the curry leaves and onion and fry until these are golden. Add the ginger paste and chillies and fry for two or three minutes. Add the tomato, all the ground spices, pork and salt.

Cook over a moderate to high flame, stirring and folding the meat in the sauce quite often, until all the paste has been absorbed; it will take 10–15 minutes. If it is absorbed sooner than this, you might need to add a splash of water and continue until you can see the masala release some oil.

Add enough water to the pan to cover the pork by 1cm; bring to a boil. Cover, reduce the heat and simmer gently for 45–55 minutes, or until the pork is tender; give the pan an occasional stir and add some water if it is getting dry. Uncover and cook off any excess water over a high heat, the sauce should be creamy. Stir in the tamarind, taste and adjust the seasoning. Serve sprinkled with fresh coconut (if using).

serves 4

2/3 tsp mustard seeds
1.5cm cinnamon stick, broken up
4 cloves
4 fat garlic cloves
15g ginger, peeled weight
1 rounded tbsp raisins
5 tbsp vegetable oil
10 fresh curry leaves
1 onion, finely chopped
1–3 green chillies, whole but pierced
1 largish tomato, blended or
    chopped
½ tsp turmeric
1½ tsp ground coriander
½ tsp ground cumin
½ tsp black pepper
400g shoulder of pork, diced into
    2.5–4cm cubes
salt, to taste
½–2/3 tsp tamarind paste, or to taste
a large handful of grated coconut,
    to serve (optional, see recipe
    introduction)

creamy, nutty lamb curry with dried figs

This fabulous dish has a wonderful warmth and flavour of whole spices. I have lightened it a little by replacing some of the cream that would normally be used with milk. I like the figs and pistachios for a burst of sublime, complementary flavours, but it doesn't really need the embellishment. I leave it to you; you can leave them out or choose to top off the dish with toasted flaked almonds, cashews or pine nuts instead. You can also stir in a little coconut cream at the end. Serve with rice or Naan (see page 155).

60g cashew nuts
200ml whole milk
5 tbsp vegetable oil
3 small onions, sliced
6 large garlic cloves
20g ginger, peeled weight
160g plain full-fat yogurt (not too
    sour, if it is add a little less)
salt, to taste
500g diced leg or shoulder of lamb
7.5cm cinnamon stick
6 cloves
7 green cardamom pods
2 blades mace
2 bay leaves
1–3 green chillies, whole but pierced
    (optional)
1½ tsp ground coriander
4 tbsp double cream, or to taste
1–1¼ tsp garam masala, or to taste
6 large dried ready-to-eat figs, halved
    or quartered (optional)
handful of pistachios, shelled and
    blanched (see page 36), or flaked
    almonds

Soak the cashew nuts in the milk for 10 minutes, then blend them together until smooth and set aside.

Heat 4 tbsp of the oil in a non-stick saucepan. Add the onions and fry gently for 10–12 minutes, until soft and translucent. Remove two-thirds of the onions, set aside, and continue to fry the rest until well browned. Remove and set these aside separately. Put any residual oil into a small bowl. Give the pan a wipe with kitchen paper.

Blend the soft, pale onions with the garlic, ginger and yogurt to a smooth paste; season. If you have time, marinate the lamb in this mixture for at least one hour; ideally, cover the dish and refrigerate overnight.

Heat the remaining oil and any residual oil (from cooking the onion), add the whole spices and bay leaves and allow them to sizzle for 10 seconds. Add the lamb, marinade, green chillies and ground coriander. Bring to a boil over a moderate flame, stirring very often. Continue to cook, stirring frequently, until all the yogurt has been absorbed and the paste releases oil; the meat will start to stick to the pan.

Add enough water to cover the lamb. Bring to a boil, cover and simmer gently for 45–60 minutes, or until the lamb is tender. Stir the pot every 10–15 minutes or so, and make sure there is always some liquid in the pan. Uncover the pot and reduce the sauce in the pan until it comes just one-third of the way up the meat. Add the cashew nut paste, cream, garam masala and dried figs (if using). Bring back to a boil and simmer for three or four minutes, the sauce should be creamy. Stir in the reserved onions and sprinkle with the nuts.

serves 6

my roganjosh

Rojanjosh as we know it is a deep, rich lamb curry which doesn't bear much resemblance to the real Indian dish. I have given a recipe for roganjosh with tomatoes, as we have come to expect it to taste, in *Anjum's New Indian*, but wanted to write this more authentic version. With its yogurt and almond base, it is equally delicious and quite different. In India they use mutton or leg of baby lamb with the bone in (try spring lamb and ask the butcher to cut into large bone-in pieces). Serve with a lovely pilaf, Naan or Chapati (see pages 155 and 156).

2 black cardamom pods
8 green cardamom pods
6 cloves
5cm cinnamon stick
2 tsp cumin seeds
5–8 Kashmiri dried chillies, seeds shaken out, or chilli powder, to taste
2 dried bay leaves (if fresh, add to lamb only once it has browned)
8 large garlic cloves
25g ginger, peeled weight, cut into large pieces
7 tbsp vegetable oil
600g spring lamb or mutton, cut into large bone-in cubes
300g full-fat yogurt, stirred well
1 tbsp ground coriander
salt, to taste
¾–1 tsp garam masala
½ tsp freshly ground black pepper
1½ tsp fennel seeds, ground
2 tbsp ground almonds
1 tsp paprika, for colour (optional)
handful of chopped fresh coriander leaves

Using a spice grinder or a good mortar and pestle, grind the whole spices to a fine powder with the dried bay leaves. Separately blend together the garlic and ginger with a good splash of water until fine.

Heat the oil in a large non-stick saucepan. Add the lamb or mutton and brown well over a high flame; this will take a good eight to 10 minutes. Add the ginger-garlic paste and cook over a moderate flame, stirring constantly as the water starts to dry. Once the paste is cooked, all you will see is clear oil in the pan and the garlic will smell cooked.

Add half the yogurt and cook over a moderate to high flame, stirring constantly and quite briskly, almost folding the yogurt into the lamb until it has been fully absorbed by the meat; it will take another eight to 10 minutes. Repeat with the remaining yogurt, stirring constantly as before. Once it is boiling, simmer, stirring every now and again, until the liquid in the pan has reduced by around one-third. Now add the ground whole spices, ground coriander and salt and cook, stirring, for a few minutes more.

Cover and cook over a low flame for 30–40 minutes, or until the meat is tender, remembering that mutton will take quite a bit longer to cook than lamb. Keep an eye on the pan and give it an occasional stir; add a good splash of water if the sauce looks dry.

Add the garam masala, black pepper, fennel seed powder and ground almonds. Taste, adjust the seasoning and add paprika (if using) for a rich red colour. Cook for another minute, add the chopped coriander and serve.

serves 4–6

lamb dhansak

Dhansak is sweet, sour and always contains lentils, though you can use whichever vegetables and meat you like. Traditionally, the vegetables are cooked in the lentils and then all is pureed together, although leaving the pieces of butternut squash intact in this recipe adds texture and little morsels of sweet earthiness. The Parsi serve this with lightly sweetened pilaf: they caramelise sugar in a small pan, add water and simmer while frying whole spices in ghee. The rice is added to the spices, then the syrup, covering with enough water to cook the rice. Plain rice or any other pilaf work just as well.

Using a sturdy mortar and pestle, grind together the whole spices to a fine powder. Add the remaining powdered spices (except the garam masala) and set aside.

Heat the oil in a large saucepan. Add the onion and sauté until golden brown. Add the ginger and garlic and sauté for a minute. Now tip in the lamb and brown for three or four minutes, or until lightly seared. Stir in the spices and a splash of water and cook for two minutes more.

Add the pigeon peas and lentils, tomato, vegetables, a handful of fresh coriander and salt, stir well and add enough water to cover. Bring to a boil, cover and simmer gently for 45–55 minutes, or until the lamb is tender. Now you can decide if you want to leave the vegetables whole in a more rustic sauce, or to blend them to a smooth result. If you would prefer the latter, remove the lamb with a slotted spoon and set aside. Blend the sauce until smooth (I stick in my hand blender), then return the meat.

Stir in the tamarind, sugar, garam masala and crushed fenugreek leaves. Taste and adjust the seasoning, balancing the levels of sweet (sugar) and sour (tamarind) to your taste. Chop the remaining fresh coriander, sprinkle it over, and serve.

serves 6, can be halved

1½ tsp fennel seeds
½ tsp fenugreek seeds
⅔ tsp mustard seeds
½ star anise
¼ tsp turmeric
¼ tsp grated nutmeg
1¾ tsp ground cumin
1½ tsp ground coriander
¼ tsp chilli powder
7 tbsp vegetable oil
1 onion, sliced
15g ginger, peeled weight, roughly chopped
4 fat garlic cloves, roughly chopped
500g lamb, in large cubes
70g split pigeon peas (*toor dal*), washed well
70g red lentils (*masur dal*), washed well
1 small tomato, roughly chopped
200g butternut squash or pumpkin, peeled and cut into 5cm cubes
1 Japanese aubergine (they are small and long), or normal aubergine, cut into 6 crossways
2 handfuls of fresh coriander
salt, to taste
1 tsp tamarind paste, or to taste
1 rounded tsp sugar, or to taste
2 tsp garam masala
1 rounded tsp fenugreek leaves, crushed between your fingers

mangalorean mutton curry

This is an absolutely delicious, robust curry and the flavours are deep and complex. I like to use mutton in this dish, but lamb also works well. Ideally try and find leg of mutton or lamb with the bone in (halal shops cut meat in this way, but ask your local butcher). This is not a quick and easy curry – it is one that you commit to with love – but it is so fabulous that you'll find it is one of those dishes you always turn to when you have friends coming around. Serve with rice or Paratha (see page 157).

Place the coconut in a small pan and dry roast for a minute or two, until golden. Grind with the cumin and poppy seeds until fine; I use a spice grinder.

Heat the oil in a non-stick saucepan and fry the onion until well browned, then tip into a blender along with the fresh coriander, chillies, ginger and garlic and a small splash of water. Whizz to a fine paste. Return to the pan and sauté for six to eight minutes. Add the tomato and all the powdered and ground spices except the garam masala, salt and around 100ml water. Sauté for seven or eight minutes, until the tomatoes have become pulpy.

Add the meat and sauté in the paste for four or five minutes. The paste should have completely reduced and be clinging to the meat, while the oil should be coming out of the masala. Add enough water to come three-quarters of the way up the lamb, bring to a boil, cover and simmer for around 45–55 minutes, or until done, stirring occasionally. Remember that mutton will take considerably longer; allow 90 minutes if using that, just in case.

Uncover, stir in the tamarind and garam masala. The sauce should be lovely, creamy and homogenous by now; if necessary boil off excess water or add a little extra from the kettle, until the consistency is as you prefer. Taste and adjust the seasoning and tamarind to your taste.

serves 6, can be halved

6 tbsp unsweetened desiccated coconut
1½ tsp cumin seeds
1 rounded tbsp white poppy seeds
6 tbsp vegetable oil
1 large onion, sliced
20g fresh coriander leaves and stalks
1–3 green chillies, or to taste, stalk removed
10g fresh root ginger, peeled weight
6 fat garlic cloves
1 tomato, chopped
½ tsp turmeric
1½ tsp ground coriander
salt, to taste
600g bone-in mutton or lamb, in large cubes
½–¾ tsp tamarind paste, or to taste
1 tsp garam masala

spicy lamb, tomato and coconut curry

A really easy-to-make dish that is rich and deep in flavours, from the coast of south west India. Nearly everything is thrown into a pot and cooked until done. Taste a little both before and after the browning or 'bhunoing' process, just for you to see how it changes a dish in flavour and texture. I use ghee here as a little adds so much flavour; if you don't have any then use half oil and half butter. Serve with Indian breads.

1 tbsp coriander seeds
1 tsp cumin seeds
15 black peppercorns
5cm cinnamon stick
4 cloves
500g boneless or 600g bone-in lamb leg or shoulder, cubed
3 small onions, finely chopped
3 tomatoes, chopped
15g ginger, peeled weight, grated into a paste
8 fat garlic cloves, grated into a paste
3–6 green chillies, whole but pierced
salt, to taste
2 tbsp ghee, or vegetable oil and butter
200–300ml coconut milk, or to taste
1½ tsp lemon juice, or to taste

Using a spice grinder or a good mortar and pestle, pound the whole spices to a fine powder.

Place the lamb, 2 of the chopped onions, tomatoes, ginger, garlic, chillies, spices and salt in a large saucepan. Add 500ml water, bring to a boil, then cover and cook gently for 45–60 minutes, or until the lamb is cooked and tender. Give the pot a stir every 10 minutes or so.

After about 45 minutes, melt the ghee in a small saucepan and fry the remaining onion until well browned.

There shouldn't be too much liquid left in the pan once the lamb is cooked. Cook off any excess moisture in the pan over a high flame for six or seven minutes, stirring quite often, until the sauce has mostly been absorbed by the lamb. This bhunoing process will help homogenise the sauce and deepen the flavours. Add the browned onion and ghee.

Pour in the coconut milk and lemon juice, bring to a boil and simmer for five minutes; the sauce should be thick and creamy. Taste and adjust the seasoning, adding lemon juice or coconut milk until the dish is perfect for you, then serve.

serves 4

3 ACCOMPANIMENTS

vegetable
side dishes

simple, lightly spiced vegetables

This is a really easy dish to make and a great way of getting your vegetables in, but it does require a little patience. The end result is that all the vegetables retain their own flavour and character. I have listed those I would typically use, but you can put in any you like as long as you add one sweet vegetable. The sweet potato is really nice in this.

Heat the oil in a non-stick sauté pan or saucepan. Add the chillies and panch phoran, reduce the flame and, once the seeds stop popping, add the vegetables, salt and turmeric. Stir well to mix, cover, reduce the heat right down and cook gently, stirring often to make sure the vegetables don't stick to the pan.

Once the vegetables are tender, after 25–30 minutes, stir in the sugar and serve immediately.

serves 2–3

2 tbsp vegetable oil
1–2 dried red chillies, seeds shaken out
scant 1½ tsp panch phoran
120g sweet potato, peeled and cut into small cubes or half- or quarter-moons
2 Japanese aubergines, or normal aubergines (around 100g), in 2.5cm half-moons
handful of small cauliflower florets
100g potato, peeled and cut into 1–1.5cm cubes
50g green beans or mangetout, topped and tailed or de-stringed
70g carrots, peeled and sliced into 1cm coins
salt, to taste
¼ tsp turmeric
¾ tsp sugar

opposite serving spicy peas with ginger, *see page 150*

sweet and sour squash

A lovely side dish from Rajasthan, with a fantastic flavour and heat to it. Serve with lentils, meat or chicken curries, or even to add a twist to your Sunday roast. I like to leave the skin on my squash as it keeps the vegetable together and adds texture.

Heat the oil in a non-stick saucepan. Add the asafoetida and cook for 20 seconds. Add the fenugreek seeds and cook until brown, then add the chillies and ginger and sauté for one or two minutes. Stir in the ground coriander and turmeric along with 1 tbsp water, and cook for a minute more.

Add the squash and sauté for two minutes. Pour in 150ml water, bring to a boil, then cover and cook for around 15 minutes, until just tender.

Add the jaggery or sugar, dried mango powder and ground fennel seeds. Make sure there is enough water in the pan; the squash should be breaking down at the edges, creamy and soft and will help form the sauce along with the water and spices. The sauce will be thick and will cling to the vegetable with a little extra to mop up with your bread. If necessary, add 3–4 tbsp more water. Taste and adjust the salt, then serve.

serves 4

2 tbsp vegetable oil
pinch of asafoetida
½ tsp fenugreek seeds
2 dried red chillies, seeds shaken out
13g fresh root ginger, peeled weight, grated into a paste
2 tsp ground coriander
½ tsp turmeric
500g butternut squash, skin on, cut into large chunks
1 tbsp jaggery or brown sugar
2–2½ tsp dried mango powder
¾ tsp ground fennel seeds
salt, to taste

quick sautéed spinach with dill

A delicious, easy accompaniment to any curry, the dill adds a lovely flavour but you can leave it out if you prefer.

Steam or boil the spinach until wilted. When cool enough to handle, squeeze out the excess water.

Heat the oil and butter in a sauté pan. Add the onion and cook for a few minutes, or until softened. Add the garlic and cook gently for another minute or so, until just cooked but not coloured. Add the spinach and tomatoes, spices and seasoning. Stir-fry for five minutes, without adding any water.

Finish with the dill and lemon juice, and serve.

serves 4

400g baby spinach, washed
1 tbsp vegetable oil
20g butter
½ small onion, chopped
4 fat garlic cloves, finely chopped
6 baby tomatoes, halved
good ½ tsp ground cumin
good ½ tsp ground coriander
generous pinch of freshly ground
    black pepper
⅛ tsp turmeric
salt, to taste
1 tbsp chopped dill
1 tsp lemon juice, or to taste

stir-fried cabbage, bengal gram and coconut

Cabbage often gets passed over for more 'interesting' greens, but whenever I make this it is loved by all, so give it another try. This is a great, light stir-fry with crisp tender cabbage enlivened by the flavours of south India. If you don't have time to cook the lentils, leave them out; the dish will still be fantastic, just not as nutritionally well-balanced.

Soak the lentils, if you have time, for as long as possible. Cook by boiling in plenty of lightly salted water until just soft; it should take 35–45 minutes, less if they have been soaked. Drain and reserve.

Heat the oil in a large frying pan. Add the mustard and nigella seeds and, once the popping dies down, the dried chillies, ginger and curry leaves; cook for a further 10 seconds. Add the cabbage, turmeric and salt and stir-fry for five to six minutes, or until the cabbage is crisp yet tender. Stir in the peanuts, lentils, coconut and a little lemon juice. Taste, adjust the seasoning and lemon juice, and serve.

serves 2

25g Bengal gram, washed well
1 tbsp vegetable oil
⅓ tsp mustard seeds
¼ tsp nigella seeds
1–3 dried red chillies, whole
8g fresh root ginger, peeled weight,
    grated into a paste
10 fresh curry leaves
¼ white cabbage head, finely
    shredded
¾ tsp turmeric
salt, to taste
40g roasted peanuts, halved or
    roughly chopped
50g fresh grated coconut, or
    3–4 tbsp unsweetened
    desiccated coconut
1½ tsp lemon juice, or to taste

creamy peas, sweetcorn and spinach

A mild, creamy curry where the spinach is a lovely, velvety foil to bursts of sweetness from the peas and crisp sweetcorn, simply flavoured with cumin and dried fenugreek leaves. This can be a main course or an accompaniment. I often serve it with Naan (see page 155) or rice to complement a robust curry. It is also lovely with roast chicken, lamb or simply cooked fish.

1 good tbsp butter or vegetable oil
½ tsp cumin seeds
¾ small onion, chopped
10g fresh root ginger, peeled weight, finely chopped
2 fat garlic cloves, finely chopped
1½ tsp dried fenugreek leaves, crumbled into a powder
1–2 green chillies, whole but pierced
25g cashew nuts
40g plain yogurt
salt, to taste
freshly ground black pepper, to taste
60g spinach, shredded (or left whole if baby spinach)
2 handfuls of frozen peas
3 tbsp canned sweetcorn kernels
4 tbsp single cream
4 tbsp milk

Heat the butter or oil in a non-stick saucepan. Add the cumin and, once it has sizzled for 10 seconds, add the onion and sauté gently until really soft. Tip in the ginger, garlic, fenugreek leaves and chillies; saute for a couple of minutes until the garlic starts to colour.

Meanwhile blend together the cashews and yogurt until smooth. Add to the pan and sauté for four or five minutes, or until it is a thick paste and releasing oil. Add 250ml water, bring back to a boil, stirring constantly, then simmer, covered, for 10 minutes.

Add the salt and pepper, spinach, peas, sweetcorn, cream and milk. Cover and cook until the spinach is soft; you may need to add another splash of water but bear in mind this should be a slightly thick, creamy curry. Taste, adjust the seasoning and serve.

serves 4

green spring vegetable thoran

A quick and easy, fresh dish that is simply spiced, this goes well with most south Indian curries or even a simple piece of grilled fish. You can use any vegetables you like; this is just one possible combination.

Heat the oil in a non-stick frying pan. Add the mustard seeds and, once they are spluttering, add the curry leaves and onion; cook until the onion is soft. Add the garlic and gently sauté for one or two minutes, until it smells cooked.

Add the vegetables, turmeric, salt, coconut and chilli and enough water to cover the base of the pan by 1–1.5cm. Cook over a moderate flame for three or four minutes, or until the vegetables are cooked to your liking (I like mine to have just a little bite). By now the water should have evaporated; if not increase the heat and quickly boil off the rest. The onions and coconut should cling to the vegetables.

Sprinkle with a little extra coconut and serve.

serves 4

3 tbsp vegetable oil
1 tsp brown mustard seeds
20 fresh curry leaves
1 onion, finely chopped
2 fat garlic cloves, finely chopped
12 large asparagus stalks, woody bit snapped off, sliced diagonally into 1cm pieces
120g green beans, topped and tailed, sliced into two or three
150g broccoli or purple-sprouting broccoli, cut into small florets
1/3 tsp turmeric
salt, to taste
2–3 tbsp unsweetened desiccated coconut, plus more to serve
1/3–1/2 tsp dried red chilli flakes, or to taste

stir-fried okra

As easy as pie, this quick recipe is delicious and one I cook regularly. You taste the okra, but the spices make for really flavourful mouthfuls of a truly healthy vegetable. I feel okra goes with everything – chicken, lamb, fish and lentils – so feel free to cook this with any main course.

Heat the oil in a frying pan. Add the cumin seeds and, once they have browned, the coriander, turmeric, chilli and salt. After they have cooked gently for 10 seconds, add the okra and stir-fry over a moderate flame until it is just cooked which, in my kitchen, takes five to seven minutes for young, fresh pods (older okra will take a little longer).

Stir in the dried mango powder, taste and adjust the flavours and seasoning to suit your palate and serve.

serves 2–3, can be doubled

2 tbsp vegetable oil
1 tsp cumin seeds
1½ tsp ground coriander
¼ tsp turmeric
⅛–¼ tsp chilli powder
salt, to taste
200g okra, wiped with damp kitchen paper, topped, tailed and sliced into 1cm pieces
⅛ tsp dried mango powder, or to taste

spicy peas with ginger

A lovely, easy dish that I often make when I have people around, both because everyone likes peas and because my mother made them for her dinner parties. We call this recipe *chat-patta*, a term which means spicy, salty and sour, all flavours that go really well with sweet peas.

Heat the oil in a saucepan, add the cumin seeds and, once they've sizzled for 10 seconds and darkened, the ginger and green chillies; sauté for a minute.

Add the coriander, cumin, salt and a splash of water and give the pot a stir. Once the water has evaporated, stir in the peas and, once they are well coated in the spices, cover and cook on a gentle flame for 10–12 minutes. I like them slightly wrinkled as I feel they have a little more flavour that way. Stir in the dried mango powder and garam masala, taste, adjust the seasoning and serve sprinkled with chopped coriander.

serves 4–6

2½ tbsp vegetable oil
2 tsp cumin seeds
20g fresh root ginger, peeled weight, finely chopped or cut into fine julienne
2 green chillies, whole but pierced
1¾ tsp ground coriander
1 good tsp ground cumin
salt, to taste
400g green peas, fresh or frozen and defrosted
⅔ tsp dried mango powder, or to taste
⅓ tsp garam masala
handful of fresh chopped coriander

cumin-crusted sautéed potatoes

I was thinking aloud with some friends about which quick potato dish I should give in this chapter and everyone pointed to these. This is really easy and quick, extremely moreish and very versatile. It could accompany a whole host of non-Indian dishes, even roast chicken. The dried mango powder is to add sourness, but if you don't have any you can add a little lemon juice or chopped tomato instead. The fresh coriander is quite important as it really lifts and enlivens the flavours.

450g potatoes, peeled
3½ tbsp vegetable oil
2 tsp cumin seeds
2 tsp ground coriander
⅓ tsp turmeric
1 rounded tsp ground cumin
¾ tsp garam masala
¼–½ tsp chilli powder, or to taste
1 tsp dried mango powder, or
    to taste
salt, to taste
large handful of fresh, chopped
    coriander

Halve the potatoes and boil them in salted water until just tender. Drain.

Heat the oil in a large frying pan. Add the cumin seeds and, once they have browned, remove the pan from the heat and add all the remaining spices and the salt. Stir to mix, return to the heat and cook for 20 seconds.

Add the potatoes and coat well in the spices. Sauté gently for five or six minutes, or until you have some brown, crusty bits, then add the fresh coriander and toss once again. Taste and adjust the seasoning, chilli and dried mango powder until you are happy with the balance, then serve.

serves 4–6

simply spiced lotus root

Most of us associate lotus root with the crisp yet flavourless spoke-like shapes found in Chinese stir-fries. But lotus root is much loved in India; the lotus is almost the national flower and is hugely symbolic. I have seen lotus root cooked in many ways, some fry it like crisps and others make it into koftas to go in a curry. This is my favourite way of eating it. The best place to find good-quality lotus roots is still in Chinese stores.

Place the lotus root in a large saucepan, cover with lots of water, season well and bring to a boil, then cover and cook until crisp but tender; it should take 12–15 minutes. Drain and leave in the colander.

Heat the oil in a wide, large non-stick pan. Add the gram flour and roast over a gentle flame for two or three minutes, stirring constantly, until it smells and tastes cooked. Add the powdered spices and salt and stir for a minute.

Add the lotus root and stir-fry gently for another four or five minutes, making sure the pieces are all well coated with the spices. Taste and adjust the seasoning, sprinkle over the chopped coriander and serve.

serves 4–5

500g lotus root, cleaned, peeled and
   sliced diagonally into 1cm pieces
salt, to taste
2½ tbsp vegetable oil
60g gram flour
1 rounded tsp garam masala
1 level tbsp dried mango powder
½–¾ tsp chilli powder
½ tsp turmeric
1¾ tbsp ground coriander
2 tsp ground cumin
large handful of chopped fresh
   coriander

breads
and rice

instant naan

Naan is our favourite restaurant bread, soft with a few dark, crisp spots that come from cooking in a super-hot tandoor oven. You can get really good results at home and, once you start making these, it is hard to stop! They are delicious and you can tailor them to your own tastes. Here is a very quick recipe with three of my favourite variations. Feel free to use the basic recipe and create your own toppings.

300g plain flour, plus more to dust
¾ tsp baking powder
½ tsp bicarbonate of soda
½ tsp salt
1½ tsp sugar
4 tbsp milk
4 tbsp plain yogurt
15g butter, melted, plus more for brushing

Preheat the oven to its highest setting (mine goes up to 275°C). Place a baking sheet on the uppermost shelf to heat through.

Mix together all the dry ingredients. Make a well in the middle and add your wet ingredients with 85–90ml of water. Bring together with your hands into a dough. Knead quickly until smooth.

Roll out into 0.75cm-thick naan breads - trying to achieve that characteristic teardrop shape - using a little more flour. Pat off any excess flour and place the breads on the hot baking sheet (you will need to do this in two batches). Cook for two to four minutes, or until there are brown spots on the upper surface. Brush with the extra melted butter, which helps to soften and brighten the surface, and serve hot.

makes 6 medium naan

caramelised onion Heat 2 tbsp vegetable oil and fry 1 sliced onion until soft. Scatter over the top of the naan before cooking.

garlic and coriander butter Crush 1 large garlic clove and add to a small saucepan with 2 tbsp butter. Melt the butter. Stir in 2 tbsp chopped fresh coriander and brush over the cooked naan.

seeded Press 1 rounded tsp of nigella or sesame seeds, or 1 rounded tbsp pumpkin seeds, or any other seeds you like (try black onion or poppy seeds) evenly into the upper surface of the breads before baking.

chapati/roti/phulka

These are all different names for the same basic, everyday wholewheat flatbreads. They are soft, puff up when cooked and, if you have a gas cooker, become a little crisp on the underside. Don't worry about not rolling a perfect circle, practice makes perfect, just keep giving the bread quarter turns for an even thickness. You can find chapati (*atta*) flour in most large supermarkets but, if you can't get hold of any, use equal quantities of wholewheat and plain flour instead. These can be made in advance and reheated, wrapped in foil, in a medium oven. I don't season this bread as it is used to mop up well-seasoned sauces, but you can add salt if you like.

300g chapati flour (or half wholewheat and half plain flour), plus more to dust
salt (optional)
200-240ml water

Sift the flour and salt (if using) into a bowl and make a well in the centre. Slowly drizzle in most of the water and, using your hand, draw the flour into the centre, mixing all the time. You may not need all the water. The dough should be slightly sticky and will firm up as you knead it. Knead for eight to 10 minutes, or until it is elastic. Place in a bowl, cover with a damp tea towel and leave for 30 minutes in a warm area, or at room temperature in the summer.

Divide the dough into 10 equal portions and roll into golf ball-sized pieces; cover again. Flour a work surface and rolling pin. Roll each ball into 12.5–15cm circles. The best way to do this is to keep rolling in one direction, regularly giving the dough a quarter turn to get a round shape.

Heat a tava or frying pan until hot. Toss the chapati from one hand to the other to remove excess flour, and place on the tava. Reduce the heat to moderate and cook until small bubbles appear on the underside, about 10–20 seconds, then flip. Cook this side until it has small dark beige spots.

Now, using tongs, place the bread directly on the gas flame. It will puff up immediately and, 10 seconds later, dark spots will appear. Turn the bread with tongs, leave for a few seconds more, then wrap in foil and keep warm in a low oven while you make the rest.

If you only have an electric cooker, press down gently on the cooked bread in the pan; as you press one area the rest should puff up. Then tackle the next bit. This way the bread should puff up all over.

makes 10, can be doubled

paratha, many ways

These flatbreads are absolutely delicious, flaky and slightly crisp. The minted type go really well with lamb curries. These are not as heavy as store-bought or restaurant varieties.

200–220ml water
300g chapati flour (*atta*), plus more to dust
a small bowl of vegetable oil, ghee or melted butter
salt, to taste

Mix the water into the flour, kneading until smooth. Divide into 10 balls. Heat a tava, flat griddle pan or frying pan. Take a ball of dough and roll it into a 15cm circle, using a little extra flour. Spread with ¾ tsp oil, ghee or butter, sprinkle evenly with a little salt and flour. Roll into a very tight log (Swiss-roll style). Then, with your palms, roll this log a bit longer, coil it tightly and pat down into a disc. Flour both sides and roll out again into a 15–17.5cm circle.

Pat off excess flour and place the paratha on the hot pan. Cook until light brown spots appear underneath, around 10–15 seconds. Turn over and spread with ¾ tsp more oil, butter or ghee (I use the back of the spoon I drizzled it over with). Once the underside has browned in spots, turn again and repeat with another ¾ tsp. oil.

Now, cut small slashes over the bread to help it crisp up. Turn again and repeat the slashes. Cook the remaining breads and serve hot.

makes 10

my favourite variations

spicy Sprinkle a pinch of both carom seeds and chilli powder over the breads with the salt.

mint Sprinkle ¾ tsp dried mint over the breads with the salt.

onion, coriander and green chilli As you knead, add a handful of chopped fresh coriander, 1 small, finely chopped onion, 2 green chillies, deseeded and sliced, 1½ tsp nigella seeds and ½ tsp salt. Don't make the rolled layers, just cook in the pan with the oil, ghee or butter as above.

a quick and easy variation You don't need to make the layers, you can just add ½ tsp salt to the dough and cook using the oil as above.

really easy bhaturas

These are lovely, fluffy, flaky breads that have been fried but don't feel at all heavy. The authentic recipe takes a lot longer to make and requires four hours of fermenting time, so my family have been using this quick way for years. They take just seconds to make and everyone loves them. Try them with Southern Potato Curry (see page 49), Tangy Chickpea Curry (see page 55) or in fact any other dish! They are truly delicious.

200g plain flour, plus more to dust
⅔ tsp salt
1 tsp sugar
¼ tsp fast-action yeast (optional)
140ml sparkling water
1 tsp vegetable oil, plus more to fry

Put the flour into a bowl and mix in the salt, sugar and yeast (if using), then pour in the sparkling water. Bring together with your hands until you have a dough, then knead until it is smooth and soft and doesn't have any cracks. Smear with the 1 tsp oil, put into a bowl and leave to rest for 30 minutes.

Divide the dough into 8 equal balls. Spoon 5 tbsp of the extra flour on to a small plate.

Flatten one ball and pat both sides in the flour. Roll out into thin 0.25–0.5cm-thick circles or ovals. Heat up about 20cm oil in a large open pan - a karahi or wok is ideal - until just smoking.

Place the bread straight into the hot oil and hold it down with a slotted spoon for five or six seconds, as it will try to rise and will puff up. Turn over; the underside should be golden. Cook this side for another few seconds, or until golden on both sides. Remove from the oil and blot off excess oil on kitchen paper. Serve, or keep them hot while you make the rest. Serve hot.

makes 8 medium breads

perfect boiled rice

Rice is one of the simplest and quickest grains to cook, yet so many people are afraid to tackle it, fearing stodgy or wet grains. The way to achieve great fluffy rice is actually really easy. This is how we have always made it in my family; it is foolproof. We are advised to discard leftover rice within a day of making it – as the bacteria in rice increases at a really fast rate – and to make sure it is always properly reheated.

50–60g good-quality basmati rice per person

Wash the rice really well in several changes of water, until the water runs clear, showing that all the starch has been removed. Place in a large, deep saucepan and cover with water to come at least 15-20cm above the level of the rice, depending on how much you are making. Bring to a boil and simmer fast (as you would for pasta) for seven to eight minutes. Taste a grain; it should be cooked through, if not wait a minute then check again.

Turn off the heat, pour the rice into a sieve, drain off all the water, then tip the rice back into the pan. Cover, and leave to steam for eight to 10 minutes.

aromatic rice pilaf

The simple yellow pilaf served in most Indian restaurants. It is lightly flavoured and a lovely accompaniment to any curry.

220g basmati rice, well washed
2 good tbsp ghee (or 1 tbsp butter and 2 tbsp vegetable oil)
1 rounded tsp cumin seeds
10cm cinnamon stick
1 bay leaf
4 green cardamom pods
4 cloves
1 smallish onion, sliced
½ tsp turmeric
salt, to taste

Tip the rice into a large bowl, cover with water and leave to soak. Heat the ghee in a saucepan. Add the cumin, cinnamon, bay leaf, cardamom pods and cloves and allow to sizzle for 10–15 seconds, or until the cumin is aromatic. Add the onion and cook until it's turning golden at the edges.

Add the drained rice, turmeric and salt and cook for a minute, stirring. Add 400ml water, then taste the water and adjust for salt. Bring to a boil, cover, reduce the heat to its lowest setting and cook undisturbed for 12–13 minutes. Check a grain, it should be cooked. Turn off the heat and serve when you are ready to eat.

serves 4

southern lemon and cashew nut rice

A lovely, fragrant rice which is perfect with coconut curries, as the lemon cuts through the sweet, creamy taste.

Place the rice in a saucepan with enough water to come at least 20cm above the level of the rice, bring to a boil and simmer for seven or eight minutes. Try a grain, it should be soft, if not cook for another minute and taste again. Turn off the heat, pour the rice into a sieve, drain off all the water, then tip the rice back into the pan. Cover, and leave undisturbed for five to eight minutes.

Heat the oil in a large non-stick frying pan and add the cashew nuts. Fry until golden, then remove and place on kitchen paper to blot off the excess oil. Add the mustard seeds to the pan and, once they have popped, add the lentils and chillies and stir-fry until the lentils darken and take on a reddish colour, but before they turn brown.

Add the ginger, turmeric, salt and 2 tbsp water and cook for 40 seconds. Pour in the lemon juice and cook for another minute before adding the rice, coconut and chopped coriander. Stir with a fork to mix well. Taste, adjust the seasoning and serve.

serves 4

220g basmati rice, well washed
4 tbsp vegetable oil
1 handful raw cashew nuts, split in half
1 tsp mustard seeds
1 tbsp split Bengal gram
2–4 dried red chillies, whole
6g fresh root ginger, chopped
$\frac{1}{3}$ tsp turmeric
salt, to taste
3½ tbsp lemon juice, or to taste
3 tbsp grated fresh coconut, or 2 tbsp unsweetened desiccated coconut
handful of chopped fresh coriander

pea and carrot pilaf

A colourful dish that goes with everything. You can make it just with peas, just carrots, or even add chopped green beans.

Place the rice in a saucepan and pour in water to come 20cm above the level of the rice. Bring to a boil and simmer for seven or eight minutes. Try a grain - it should be soft - if not cook for a minute and taste again. Pour into a sieve, drain, then tip back into the pan. Cover and leave for five to eight minutes.

Heat the oil in a wide frying or sauté pan and add the cumin seeds, cinnamon, cloves, bay leaves and cardamom. Cook until the cumin is aromatic, around 20 seconds. Add the onion and stir-fry until just soft. Add the carrots, peas and salt, then a splash of water. Cover and cook for two or three minutes. The carrots should retain a little bite. Uncover the pan, there should be no water left (if there is cook it off over a high heat). Add the rice and garam masala and stir with a fork to mix well. Taste, adjust the seasoning and serve.

serves 4

220g basmati rice, well washed
4 tbsp vegetable oil
1 rounded tsp cumin seeds
10cm cinnamon stick
4 cloves
2 bay leaves
2 black cardamom pods
1 small onion, sliced
½ large carrot, cut into 1cm cubes
90g peas
salt, to taste
½ tsp garam masala

creamy saffron and nut rice

A rich dish; the nuts and raisins add texture and sweetness.

Tip the rice into a bowl, cover with water and leave to soak. Heat the milk and cream until hot and pour into a jug. Sprinkle in the saffron. Set aside.

Heat 1 tbsp ghee in a saucepan, add the almonds and cashews and cook until golden. Pour into a bowl and add the pistachios. Add the remaining ghee to the pan and, once hot, the whole spices. Once the cumin is aromatic, add the onion and raisins and cook until the onion is soft and turning golden at the edges. Stir in the rice. Add enough water to the saffron jug to make a total of 400ml and pour it in with the nuts. Add salt to taste. Bring to a boil then reduce the heat to really low, cover and cook for 11–12 minutes. Check the rice is cooked, then turn off the heat and leave to steam, covered, for eight to 10 minutes. Serve hot.

serves 4

220g basmati rice, well washed
5 tbsp milk
1 tbsp double cream
good pinch of saffron
3 tbsp ghee (or 2 tbsp butter and
    1½ tbsp vegetable oil)
30g blanched almonds, halved
30g cashew nuts, halved
30g unsalted pistachios
10cm cinnamon stick
5 cloves
1 rounded tsp cumin seeds
1 black cardamom pod
3 green cardamom pods
1 small onion, halved and sliced
3 tbsp raisins
salt, to taste

salads and
raitas

quick carrot salad

You can put this together in an instant, and it's great for cleansing the palate during a rich meal.

Coarsely grind the peanuts in a good mortar and pestle.

Toss the grated carrots with the ground peanuts, salt, sugar, lemon juice and chopped coriander.

Heat the oil in your smallest pan until hot. Add the mustard seeds and cover, as they will splutter. As they reduce their spluttering, pour them over the salad and toss to mix well. Taste, adjust the seasoning and serve.

serves 2–3

2 tsp dry roasted peanuts
2 large carrots, peeled and coarsely grated
salt, to taste
½ tsp sugar
1¾ tsp lemon juice, or to taste
small fistful of chopped fresh coriander leaves
1 tbsp vegetable oil
1 tsp brown mustard seeds

indian chopped salad (*kachumber*)

A wonderfully crunchy salad that is great with any curry.

Chop the tomatoes into small dice. Slice the cucumber lengthways, discard the seeds and cut into small cubes the same size as the tomatoes. Do the same with the radish.

Toss together all the vegetables and chillies (if using), season, stir through the lemon juice, roasted cumin powder and chopped coriander, and serve, or keep at room temperature until you are ready to eat.

serves 4

2 ripe vine tomatoes
120g cucumber (I keep the skin on)
4 small radishes
½ small onion, finely chopped
1–2 green chillies, seeded and chopped (optional)
salt, to taste
1 tbsp lemon juice, or to taste
⅓ tsp roasted cumin powder (see page 55)
handful of chopped fresh coriander leaves

warm tandoori mushroom, spinach and chickpea salad

A lovely salad with lots of flavours and textures that takes only 10 minutes to make. The mushrooms are marinaded then grilled to intensify their flavours, becoming wonderfully deep-tasting. The roasted cumin powder in the dressing is optional so, if you are in a hurry, you can leave it out.

Mix together all the ingredients for the marinade. Keep small shiitake and oyster mushrooms whole, but halve the others. Cut the chestnut mushrooms into 1.5cm slices. Toss the mushrooms in the marinade, making sure each piece is coated, then set aside for 30 minutes.

Heat your grill to high and grill the mushrooms for three to four minutes each side, or until lightly charred; the shiitake and oyster mushrooms will take three minutes and the chestnut mushrooms will take an extra minute each side.

Meanwhile, whisk together the ingredients for the dressing with 1 tsp water.

Place the baby spinach in a bowl, add the hot mushrooms, chickpeas, walnuts and dressing, season well and toss to coat. Serve immediately.

serves 4 as an accompaniment

for the tandoori marinade
2 fat garlic cloves, grated into a paste
8g fresh root ginger, grated into a paste
½ tsp chilli powder
¾ tsp salt, or to taste
¾ tsp garam masala
¾ tsp ground cumin
2½ tbsp lemon juice
5 tbsp olive oil

for the salad
300g mixed mushrooms (shiitake, oyster and chestnut), cleaned
100g baby spinach, well washed
200g canned chickpeas, drained and rinsed
large handful of walnuts, lightly crushed
lots of freshly ground black pepper, to taste

for the dressing
1⅓ tbsp cider, sherry or white wine vinegar
3 tbsp extra-virgin olive oil
good ½ tsp Dijon mustard
½ red onion, finely sliced
⅓ tsp roasted cumin powder (see page 55, optional)

top quick carrot salad, *see page 165*
bottom warm tandoori mushroom, spinach and chickpea salad

mango raita

A lovely sweet, sour and lightly spiced raita which will help temper the heat of hot curries.

Slice the cheeks from the mangoes. Peel and cut the flesh into small cubes (see below for techniques).

Mix together the yogurt, coconut and sugar until the sugar has 'melted'. Add the mango and its juices, a little salt to taste and the chopped coriander.

Heat the oil in a small saucepan, add the mustard seeds and cook until they have popped. Stir into the raita, taste and adjust the seasoning. Serve sprinkled with a little chilli powder (if using).

serves 4

2 small, sweet mangoes (ripe but not soft)
400g plain yogurt
2 tbsp unsweetened desiccated coconut
1½ tsp sugar, or to taste (depends on the sweetness of the mango and sourness of the yogurt)
salt, to taste
a good handful of chopped fresh coriander
1 tsp vegetable oil
½ tsp mustard seeds
¼ tsp chilli powder (optional)

cutting a mango

There are two ways to cut a mango:

The first is to cut the cheeks from the mango then halve them lengthways. Slice the flesh from the skin with a knife, trying to avoid cutting away too much flesh, and cut it into small cubes. You can then tackle the 'wedges' on the sides, though it is hard to get clean slices here as the flesh around the stone can be quite fibrous. I try to get what I can.

The other way is to cut the cheeks from the mango, then slice straight lines into the flesh all the way down to the skin. Give the cheeks a quarter turn and slice again to create squares. Now push the cheek inside out and cut off the squares. Tackle the sides in the same way as above.

top crispy okra raita, see page 171
middle mango raita
bottom cucumber and mint raita, see page 171

tomato, onion and cucumber raita

This is my favourite raita and the one we eat the most.

Stir all the ingredients together and season to taste.

serves 4

1 small vine tomato, chopped into 1cm dice
90g cucumber, peeled and chopped into 1cm dice
½ small red onion, finely chopped
large handful of chopped fresh coriander
¾ tsp roasted cumin powder (see page 55)
⅓ tsp chilli powder
400g plain yogurt, whisked until smooth
salt, to taste

mint and garlic yogurt

This is a yogurt that I love. It isn't very Indian, but tastes great with Indian food so I wanted to include it for all the garlic lovers like myself.

Mix all the ingredients together, taste, adjust the seasoning and serve.

serves 4–5

400g full- or half-fat Greek yogurt
1 garlic clove, grated into a paste
salt, to taste
10 large mint leaves, shredded

apple, orange and mint raita

A lovely, refreshing raita that is perfect for those who like a hint of sweetness or fruitiness with their meal.

Using a small sharp knife, cut into the orange segments on either side of the membrane, so the segment falls out. Cut these in half and add to the yogurt.

Add all the other ingredients and stir well to mix. Taste, adjust the seasoning and serve, or chill until required.

serves 4–6

1 small orange, peeled
400g plain yogurt
1 small, crunchy apple, cut into 1cm dice (peeled or skin on, you decide)
large sprinkling of shredded mint leaves
1 scant tsp roasted cumin powder (see page 55)
salt, to taste
sprinkling of chilli powder (optional)

cucumber and mint raita

A refreshing raita that is really versatile; it's lovely with Indian food but also great with barbecues. I even eat it with my baked potato; delicious and healthy. It's always best to measure out mint leaves, even small quantities, as they can be strong and may otherwise overpower a dish.

200g cucumber (½ a large one)
400g thick plain yogurt
salt and freshly ground black pepper, to taste
8g mint leaves, shredded
¾ tsp roasted cumin powder (see page 55)

Grate the cucumber on the coarse side of your box grater. Squeeze out all the excess water and place the cucumber in a large bowl.

Add all the remaining ingredients and stir well to mix. Serve cold.

serves 4

crispy okra raita

A delightful raita with the subtle flavours of the coast. The crisp okra provides texture to this thick, slightly sweet dish.

400g Greek yogurt
4 tsp sugar, or to taste
salt, to taste
vegetable oil, to deep-fry
12 large okra, topped, tailed and sliced into 1cm rounds
⅓ tsp brown mustard seeds
12 curry leaves

Stir the yogurt until smooth and loosen with 3-4 tbsp water. Stir in the sugar and a little salt.

Heat 5cm oil in a small saucepan, add the okra and fry gently until crisp and just turning colour; stirring occasionally. Spoon out and place on a kitchen paper-lined plate. Toss in a little seasoning.

Pour out all but 1 tsp of oil from the pan. Reheat the oil and add the mustard seeds. Once the noise in the pan starts to die down, add the curry leaves and turn off the heat. Pour into the yogurt and stir well to mix. Taste and adjust sugar and salt to taste, it should be sweet rather than salty.

When you are ready to eat, stir in most of the okra and sprinkle with the rest.

serves 4–5

spices 101

Spices were once more valuable than gold, and their worth in the kitchen remains priceless. They can be seeds (mustard), fruits (mango), roots (turmeric), barks (cinnamon) or even flower stamens (saffron). You need to know the different qualities of each to be a truly excellent curry cook. Some are earthy, others sharp; they can be musty, citrussy, tangy, peppery, pungent, hot or even herb-like. Here's the essential guide to navigating them. Many will require a trip to an Asian store, or a little shopping online (see bottom right). But if you cook curries regularly – and you probably do if you've bought this book – you only need to shop for spices every six months, as they will last well in an airtight container, in a cool, dark place.

common ground spices

Chilli powder *(lal mirch)* The heat of this varies from one batch to another. Generally speaking, the darker the shade, the milder the heat. The mildest is Kashmiri chilli powder *(degi mirch* in Hindi). Chilli powder will add wonderful colour and heat to your dishes but little flavour, unlike fresh chillies.

Coriander *(sabut dhania)* These large, pale, spherical seeds are mild and almost citrussy in taste, with a fabulous aroma. Once powdered, they are one of the most commonly used spices in Indian food, rounding off and softening stronger flavours.

Cumin *(jeera)* This very familiar spice is used all around the world. You'll find it in Mexican, North African and Malaysian dishes, as well as in Indian food. It is earthy and savoury and can be fried or dry-roasted to a darker shade with a nutty loveliness.

Garam masala A famous blend of warming spices that differs from home to home but usually contains cloves, black and green cardamom and cinnamon as well as bay leaves and black peppercorns. Milder mixes will also contain coriander and cumin. It can be added either towards the end of cooking for a real punch of aroma, or closer to the beginning for a more rounded, subtle taste.

Turmeric *(haldi)* This vibrant, mustard-yellow powder is essential in Indian cooking. It is prized both for its colour and for its fantastic medicinal properties. It should be used sparingly as the subtle, musty flavour can be unpleasant in large quantities.

common whole spices

Black cardamom *(badi elaichi)* These large, woody pods have a lovely smoky aroma and are loved by many north Indians. Use in lamb and chicken curries and pilafs.

Black peppercorns *(kali mirch)* This spice needs little introduction... except to say the taste and aroma of freshly ground peppercorns is so superior to shop-bought powder that the latter is not worth buying.

Brown mustard seeds *(rai)* When fried in hot oil, these small brown seeds release a nutty, mild mustard flavour. When powdered, they have a stronger taste. When you grind this spice, be careful to not overwork it or it can become bitter. I very briefly blitz a large amount at a time in a spice blender and then store.

Cinnamon and cassia *(dal chini)* Cassia bark is similar to cinnamon and is more commonly used in India. I prefer to use both whole in my curries or pilafs. I add cassia bark in large shards but, as cinnamon is more delicate, it's best to add it in quills so it breaks up less. The two are interchangeable in Indian food.

Cloves *(laung)* Often used in small quantities in curries, these have a distinct, strong and slightly sweet flavour.

Curry leaves (*curri patta*) These are an important part of coastal food. They are highly aromatic when fresh, but lose much of their flavour when dried. You can buy them fresh in decent quantities in Indian stores and freeze them for future use; they keep perfectly.

Dried chillies Used a lot in India, especially in the areas where fresh chillies are hard to find. There are so many different types, each with its own heat and flavour profile, so be careful the first time you cook with any unfamiliar variety. If you are grinding them, break them in half crosswise and shake the seeds straight into the bin, as these hold most of the heat. You can now buy Kashmiri dried chillies in some supermarkets; these are mild with a lovely dark, rich colour. You can also buy crushed dried chillies, which can be added late in the cooking process to correct a recipe's heat level. This is a godsend if you taste a dish and find it too mild.

Fennel seeds (*saunf*) A sweet, licquorice-like spice that can either be added whole to hot oil or ground.

Fenugreek leaves (*kasturi methi*) These dried leaves have a unique savoury and pleasingly bitter flavour when you crush or crumble them into your curry. They are especially delicious in lentil and chicken dishes, or with spinach and even cauliflower.

Green cardamom (*chotti elaichi*) Gently-flavoured pods with a subtle but unmistakable aroma, used in sweet and savoury dishes, pilafs and in Indian spiced tea. Grind them either with or without their green skins (the skin has lots of flavour but is harder to grind finely).

Green chillies While most westerners think of chillies in terms of heat, I use them more for their flavour. Keeping them whole in a curry, as I tend to, means the heat stays within the chilli and you mostly get their taste. I use the Indian thin finger-like chillies that you can buy in Indian stores; they keep in the fridge for weeks. You can buy green chillies from supermarkets, but they won't have the same flavour or heat.

my top ten unusual spices

Asafoetida (*heeng*) This pungent powder makes food easier to digest; some think it tastes like cooked garlic.

Carom seeds (*ajwain*) A small, dark green seed with a flavour reminiscent of thyme. Use with fish, hard-to-digest vegetables and in some Indian breads.

Chaat masala A blend with a wealth of flavours, such as cumin, mint, carom, asafoetida, mango and ginger. It's tangy and often sprinkled over tandoori dishes.

Dried mango powder (*amchur*) Tangy but not sweet. Use it instead of lemon juice for tartness without liquid.

Dried pomegranate powder (*anardana*) The powdered seeds of a variety of pomegranate. It has a tart fruitiness that's great with chickpeas and lamb (see page 119).

Fenugreek seeds (*methre*) Hard, strong-tasting seeds, these can be bitter. Cook in hot oil until they darken well.

Nigella seeds (*kalonji*) These delicate black teardrop-shaped seeds have a peppery flavour but no heat. Lovely with seafood, vegetables, or naan bread (see page 155).

Panch phoran A Bengali mix of whole seeds including fenugreek, mustard, fennel, cumin and nigella. Often used with fish, vegetables and lentils.

Saffron (*kesar*) The dried stamen of a variety of crocus, with a delicate, musky flavour; a little goes a long way. Store it in the fridge.

Star anise (*phool chakri*) Immediately recognisable, this spice looks like the spokes of a wheel, or a flower. It has a lovely, slightly aniseed flavour and strong aroma.

www.pureindianspices.co.uk
www.steenbergs.co.uk
www.thespiceshop.co.uk

Editorial Director Anne Furniss
Creative Director Helen Lewis
Project Editor Lucy Bannell
Designer Claire Peters
Photographer Jonathan Gregson
Food Stylist Sunil Vijayakar
Props Stylist Liz Belton
Production Director Vincent Smith
Production Controller Marina Asenjo

First published in 2010 by
Quadrille Publishing Limited
Alhambra House
27-31 Charing Cross Road
London WC2H 0LS
www.quadrille.co.uk

Text © 2010 Anjum Anand
Photographs © 2010 Jonathan Gregson
Design and layout © 2010
Quadrille Publishing Limited

Cataloguing in Publication Data: a catalogue
record for this book is available from the British
Library.

ISBN 978 184400 889 6
Printed in China

I would like to thank my husband Adarsh for his support and understanding and for inspiring me, through his own work ethic, to try ever harder to achieve my goals.

Thank you to my family for being there for me and understanding that when I write a book I often neglect other parts of my life! I would also like to thank my friends for cheering me on despite the fact that I temporarily disappeared from their lives, and for knowing that I still love them and miss them.

Thank you Shy for looking through my recipes, pointing out what's missing and reminding me about what other people like to eat and cook. You are always my first port of call when I need clarity.

Thank you Shaleen for your time and patience and for offering your insight about what people want to eat.

I would like to thank my friend and agent Heather Holden Brown, who was the one to say I needed to write a book on curries containing all her - and Britain's - favourite dishes. She was right, of course. I would like to express my continued gratitude to the team at Quadrille who are really supportive and brought this book to life, as well as to Jonathan Gregson for his beautiful, rich photography, and to Sunil Vijayakar, for making the food look so good.

Thank you to chef Kunal at the Leela Hotel in Delhi, who taught me some of his curry recipes. I really enjoyed cooking with you, your food is delicious and has a lot of love infused with the flavours. I hope your dreams come true. And thank you so much to Zareer Lallakakka for his lovely warm hospitality and insight into Parsi food and flavours. Zareer, your old-world chivalry is truly refreshing; I loved meeting you and your family. And thank you for the semolina sweet, which I did finish!